A Box Full Of Letters

For information contact: Shalako Press
P.O. Box 371, Oakdale, CA 95361-0371
http://www.shalakopress.com

ISBN: 978-0-9846811-5-0

Cover Design: Jennifer Kuhns
Cover art and illustrations: Patty Burgi Sneed
Cover format: Karen Borrelli
Editor: Judith Mitchell

PRINTED IN THE UNITED STATES OF AMERICA

A Box Full Of Letters

Dedication

To Maynard, whom I never met, but gave me inspiration and direction in the letters he wrote and sent home to his family.

Joan watched as the door to room number eight swung open and children stampeded out like a heard of wild chimpanzees. Joan, Hailey's mother, was standing with all of the other mothers waiting on the sidewalk in front of the school when Hailey picked her out of the crowd and waved. Joan waved back at Hailey and waited for her to maneuver her way through the mob of school children. Hailey rolled up to where her mother was standing, all excited and out of breath.

"Are you alright, honey? Your face is all red. How was your day?" Joan asked as she touched Hailey's cheek with the back of her hand.

Hailey brushed her mother's hand away. "Yeah, I'm fine. It was fine, but I need to ask you something."

"Hold up a second," Joan interrupted. "Let's get you loaded into the van first. I want to give you my full attention." Once Joan had Hailey in the van and had started strapping the wheelchair securely to the floor with the tie downs, she gave Hailey the go ahead. "Okay, ask away."

Hailey, with her most serious expression, began the speech she had been practicing in her head for the last hour. "Okay, so, can I have friends over? When can I have friends over? Can they come over tomorrow, or do we have to wait until this weekend? I know I have to clean my room, but I can do that tonight and…"

Joan stopped what she was doing and held her hand up in front of Hailey's face. "Whoa! Hold on there kiddo. Slow down. You're singing a totally different tune than you were this morning. You don't seem like you have butterflies in your stomach anymore."

Hailey paused in the middle of her sentence and grinned mischievously up at her mother. "Yeah, I know. At first it was weird, and I was nervous, and the other kids asked all kinds of goofy questions. Then we talked about disabilities, and me, and the teacher's big feet, and all kinds of stuff."

Hailey saw her mother start to look sad, then confused before she asked, "The teacher's feet?"

"Yeah, that's her disability," Hailey answered hurriedly, flapping her hand back and forth and shaking her head. "I'll tell you about that later. But, wait, I want to tell you about this first." She took a deep breath and began again. "So, they, ya know, the kids in my class got to know me, and I got to know them, and it was just like my old school. They started acting like I was just the same as them. They're really nice. Just like my old friends, most of them anyway," Hailey continued excitedly without taking a breath. "There's this one boy who has blue hair…"

"What!" Joan suddenly stopped what she was doing, again, and stood up in the van bumping her head on the ceiling. "Ouch!" She exclaimed, rubbing the top of her head. "Are you serious? He has blue hair?"

Surprised, Hailey started to laugh and then grabbed her mouth to stop. She didn't know if her mother was crying because she was really hurt or because she thought blue hair was funny. Hailey watched for some sign from her mother. Joan began to laugh, plopping down in the seat next to Hailey still holding onto her head. "For real? Blue hair?"

"Yeah, for real," Hailey giggled. "You'll probably get to see him soon; on account of he's a friend of another boy named Blake who lives on our street. And they'll probably want to come over when the girls come over." Hailey suddenly realized that she had created an opening to get back to her previous question. Before Joan could stand up and finish tying down the wheelchair, Hailey jumped at the chance to continue. "So, can they come over? When can they come over?"

Hailey noticed a smile creeping across her mother's face as she stood bent over tugging on the straps that secured the wheelchair to the floor of the van. "MOM!" Hailey shouted in frustration. "Are you listening? Are you thinking or what?"

Joan wiped the smile from her face and looked up at Hailey with a questioning expression. "What? I'm sorry. What were you asking me? I must have been zoning."

Totally exasperated, Hailey threw her head back and anchored her hands firmly on her hips and squealed, "Huhhhhh! Geez Mom, stop teasing me. Can my new friends come over or not?"

"Yes, they can come over! Calm down!" Hailey's mother laughed. "Let's talk about it after your dad gets home, okay? Right now help me figure out what we are going to have for dinner. We might have to go to the store or do take-out or something. I've been unpacking all day and haven't had time to think about it."

Hailey quietly pumped one arm up and down in front of her face and whispered, "Yes!" Then she answered her mom with an excited "Okay. Cool. Thanks." Hailey thought again and added, "And I'll have my room cleaned up by then."

"Yes you will," Joan returned as she looked up at Hailey in the rearview mirror with one eyebrow raised.

Hailey shot her mom a big exaggerated toothy smile that made Joan chuckle to herself. "You're welcome," she answered then continued in French, "*Ce que vous pensez de la pizza ce soir?* (how do you feel about pizza tonight). We can have Dad pick it up on his way home from work."

"Sweet!" Hailey agreed. "Pizza sounds super."

Hailey was busy cleaning her bedroom when her dad, Andrew, came home from his first day at work with a huge pizza. "Hey, I'm home!" Andrew yelled as he put the pizza in the oven. Joan had already turned it on. It was one of those take-n-bake kinds.

"Hi back to you," Joan answered as she pulled her head out of the cupboard that she was putting dishes into. "How was your day? Mine was terrific," she said as she waved her arm like a game show model toward the living room where there were still a ton of boxes in the middle of the floor and the furniture still placed haphazardly in the room.

"Mine was good." Andrew laughed and asked, "How's Hailey's day been, and where is she?"

"Good, really good, I think. She seems to have met some friends already and wants to invite them over this weekend," Joan mused.

"That's my girl," Andrew chuckled as he headed toward Hailey's room. He found her listening to her ipod and singing while she made her bed, unpacked boxes, and put things on shelves. Andrew watched as Hailey used her wheelchair to help push her furniture around the room to where she wanted it, and then use a stocking hook (stick with a hook on the end of it) to hang up her clothes. Hailey was so focused on what she was doing she didn't even hear her dad come into her room. "Hey, how was your day? Mom said you were in your room, cleaning. How come you are in here cleaning?" Andrew asked with a quizzical look on his face. "This is so not like you."

"Oh, hi Dad," Hailey answered. "I'm cleaning my room 'cause I want to have some friends over, but I can't if my room is a mess."

"Is that so?" Andrew joked.

"Well, I thought I'd have a better chance of Mom saying yes when we discuss it at dinner. Mom said we were gonna discuss it at dinner when you got home. Oh yeah, did you bring home a pizza?" Hailey spouted.

"I sure did, and your Mom is waiting for you to help in the kitchen," Andrew replied as he headed out of Hailey's room toward the living room to hook up the computer, television and stereo equipment.

"Cool!" Hailey exclaimed as she made her way to the kitchen through the café doors and up to the serving cart that she used to move things from one place to another.

She hooked the footrest on her wheelchair underneath the cart to push and grabbed onto the handle to guide the cart. Joan had already placed plates, silverware, glasses, napkins, and a pitcher of water on the cart.

"Be careful. Don't spill the water," Joan warned.

"I know, I know Mom! This is my job, remember?" Hailey answered over her shoulder as she navigated back through the swinging café doors to the dining room where she set the table with three place settings. When Hailey returned to the kitchen, her mom was already standing with the cooked pizza.

"Here ya go," Joan said, placing the pizza on the cart.

"Mmmm," Hailey hummed. "That smells really good!"

"Why don't I get this while you go get your dad for dinner," Joan offered, taking the serving cart from Hailey and heading to the dining room as Hailey followed.

"Okay, sure, give me the impossible mission," Hailey joked and yelled, "Dad, dinner is ready!"

When Andrew didn't respond, Joan said, "I could have done that. You have to *GO* get him. Don't just yell." Smiling, she added, "Don't come back without him."

Hailey found her dad sitting in the middle of the floor surrounded by a huge pile of wires and cables. The television was on and the controller was in his hand. Andrew was concentrating on programming the DVR when Hailey rolled up behind him. "Hey, Dad, dinner is ready."

When Andrew didn't respond, Hailey tried again. "Dad, did you hear me? Dinner is ready." She waited again, and when Andrew still did not answer, she decided to drive up closer and yelled, "DAD, DINNER IS READY!"

Hailey watched as he jumped up and hit his head on an entertainment center shelf. She started to giggle and jerked the joystick on her wheelchair so she could back up out of the way. "Sorry, Dad, I didn't mean to scare you. I just came in to tell you that dinner is ready."

Andrew absent-mindedly rubbed his head as he turned and looked at Hailey. "That's alright sweetie," he answered. "I'll live. You know me, I get all involved in something and everything else kind of disappears. I'll be there in just a minute."

Hailey didn't move as Andrew bent over and began to fiddle with the knobs and dials in front of him. A few seconds later he realized that Hailey was still sitting in the same place and looked at her blankly. He attempted to say something, but Hailey threw her hands in front of her face and scolded, "I don't think so, Dad. Mom said not to come back without you. I'm kinda hungry, so can we go already?"

Andrew gave Hailey a steely look and took a step back with both hands in front of himself. "Okay, okay, let's go," he conceded as he put down his tools and added with a chuckle, "We can't fight the establishment, I suppose."

Andrew draped an arm around Hailey's shoulders as the two of them headed for the dining room. Unexpectedly, Hailey stopped and turned to look at her dad. Halted by Hailey's sudden stop, he saw the puzzled look on his daughter's face.

"What?" Andrew asked as he once again rubbed his head.

"What does that mean?" Hailey questioned.

"What does what mean?" Andrew answered.

"That thing about the establishment," Hailey continued.

Hailey watched as her dad appeared to be thinking of an answer to her question. He stood there with his thumb and his finger on his chin looking up at the ceiling like he always did when he was trying to come up with an answer to one of her questions. She wondered if all electronic geeks did that; pondered. Once, along time ago, when she had asked him something and had to wait for an answer, that's what he said

7

he was doing, pondering. He said that pondering was like figuring something out, and in his job as a computer electronics technician, he had to figure out a lot of stuff. Hailey's dad pondered a lot.

"Let's see," Andrew began, "it means that things are done a certain way because someone, in earlier times or in the past, or someone very important or powerful, made the decision that that is the way it is supposed to be done. That is the establishment. Usually rules, laws, or the government are what people are talking about when they talk about the establishment. It is pretty much what and how people think about things. In this case, your mom is the establishment. She said dinner was ready, and if you want to get fed you don't argue. You don't fight the establishment."

Hailey sat quietly for a long moment. She was thinking about what her dad had just explained. "If that was true, Dad, you wouldn't be able to talk Mom into letting you eat dinner in front of the TV when football is on," Hailey commented and then continued, "I think you're wrong. I think you can ask the establishment to change the rules, to change their minds. All you have to do is show them how something else might be better or work better...or at least be okay to do even though it's different."

Hailey proudly smiled up at her dad when Andrew winked and began to shake his head up and down. She guessed that he was impressed with her come-back, her own understanding and ability to reason things out. She was pretty good at thinking of other ways to get something done. Her mom always said that's being differently-abled. She said that Hailey might not be able to walk, but was really good at doing other things, even better than other people. Even though her legs might not work, Hailey knew she had a better memory than most people. Her mom always told her friends that she had a memory like an elephant.

"You might be right," Andrew agreed, looking wearily into the kitchen for Joan, "but we probably shouldn't try tonight."

"She's not in there, Dad, she's already in the dining room waiting for us," Hailey prompted, pointing her thumb over her shoulder in another direction.

Andrew's eyes followed the alternative path Hailey had just hinted at and they both headed the same way. "So, how about we practice our primes while we walk to the dining room then?" Andrew coaxed. "I'll start ... 2."

"... 3, 5, 7, 11, 13," Hailey spouted, "17, 19, 23, 29, 31, 41," ending with 101 as Hailey and her dad reached her mother, patiently waiting at the table.

"It's about time," Joan reprimanded. "I was beginning to think I was going to be eating by myself tonight."

Andrew sheepishly slid into his chair and threw a quick grin at Hailey. "Sorry Mom," Hailey apologized as she rolled up to her place at the table. "You did tell me not to come back without him," she laughed.

"You're right. I did say that. You follow orders well," Hailey's mother jokingly answered. "Who's ready for pizza?"

As her mother sliced the pizza, Hailey slyly looked over at her father and smiled as she mouthed the word 'establishment.'

Hailey and her parents settled in around the dinner table eating, laughing and sharing the events of each others' day. Andrew announced that he spent his first day at his new job, as an electronics technician, meeting people and getting to know what was expected of him. Hailey knew her dad had been transferred from his old job to this new one in Iowa because the part of the company that was in this state needed someone to teach them how to troubleshoot a new computer program that was going to be released soon, and her dad knew the most about the program. It was called Suitcase 1013. She wasn't sure what it did, but it sounded cool.

Joan confirmed that she had been unpacking boxes all day and would probably be doing the same thing for weeks and weeks. Both Hailey and Andrew laughed, pretending to be sympathetic when she added, "I'm sure of it...weeks." The two of them quit laughing and their eyes got big and round when Joan continued with a smirk and a raised eyebrow, "Unless I can solicit some help from the two of you. I would kind of like to get things squared away in the next couple of days so I can look for a storefront to rent and get my shop opened."

Hailey's mom had a natural herb shop where they used to live. It was called **Natural by Burke.** She made and sold all kinds of stuff in the store that smelled really good. There were soaps, and lotions, shampoos and conditioners, lip balm and bath fizz, and even spices. Her mom had hired someone to run that store when they left California and she was going to open a second one here in Iowa. Hailey liked going into the shop to help her mom make all the cool stuff and learn about the herbs and essential oils her mom used. Her favorites were the ones that smelled like oranges and lemons.

"We are so there, Mom," Hailey assured her mother. "Aren't we, Dad?"

"You bet we are!" Andrew chimed in bobbing his head up and down, with a string of cheese from his last bite of pizza flopping up and down, too. "What ever my girls need."

Hailey pointed a finger at her dad and the mess of cheese hanging on his face. "What?" Andrew feigned surprise as he grabbed a napkin and tried to look down his own face. "Speaking of what my girls need," Andrew remembered as he attempted clean the cheese from his face, "I understand that you have something you want to discuss, but tell me about your school day first."

Hailey took a deep breath. She really wanted to ask if her new friends could come over. She was 'sooo' over talking about school. Sometimes her parents made too big of a deal about changes; not as bad as other people, but Hailey guessed that they still worried about what they called 'her well-being'. She knew they really meant 'that people weren't being mean to her' and that she felt comfortable at her new school. So, Hailey shared what she thought was the abridged version of the events of her day at her new school with her dad. She mentioned the boy bumping into her, the twins, the boy with blue hair, which made Andrew look at Joan who was shrugging her shoulders, and all of the new friends she had made. With that out of the way, Hailey ended her speech asking her most important question, "So, Dad, can I have friends over? When can I have friends over?"

Both Andrew and Joan burst out laughing at their daughter's excitement and persistence. Stunned, Hailey almost yelled, "I'm being serious!" But realizing that her parents were teasing, Hailey patiently waited for her them to stop laughing and answer her question.

After what seemed like hours to Hailey, she finally watched her dad wipe the tears out of his eyes. "I'm sorry, honey. Of course you can have friends over," he gasped out between semi-controlled giggles. "Why don't you invite them to come over on Saturday afternoon? Mom and I would love to meet your new friends, and I bet you guys might like to explore the big basement. There is a lot of old family stuff down there."

"Thank you, thank you, thank you!" Hailey stuttered happily. "I can't wait!" She hurriedly finished her dinner with a giant smile on her face. She smiled so much that her face started to hurt and when she couldn't contain herself any longer, Hailey asked to be excused from the table and for permission to use the phone to call her friends. She couldn't wait to get the ball rolling and make plans for Saturday. Joan and Andrew remained at the table for a while drinking coffee

11

and discussing their own plans for the rest of the week while occasionally stopping to listen to Hailey joyously chat with her new friends. When their cups were empty Andrew excused himself and headed back to finish setting up all of the electronics.

"By the way," Andrew added as he peeked his head back around the corner of the dining room wall, "I ordered the wheelchair lift we talked about for the basement. It should be here tomorrow. That should give me plenty of time to get it installed and working for Hailey to use on Saturday. I'm thinkin' that will be a great place for the kids to play, especially this winter. It is heated, has electricity, and there is a ton of stuff down there for them to explore, and it will give them a warm place to play during the winter time. We aren't in California anymore, Toto! Iowa has snow ya know."

"Great!" Joan returned as she too started to get up from the table. "I was wondering what I was going to do with a dozen or so kids all day in the house while I was still trying to get things organized." Then she looked around the kitchen and decided to give her daughter a break and do the evening dishes. That had been one of Hailey's chores for about the last six months. After that she spent a little while longer arranging the kitchen. When Joan finally looked at the clock it was 8:02 p.m. She walked over to where Hailey was still talking on the phone and gave her the hatchet sign by moving her hand back and forth across her neck. Hailey looked up at her mom, smiled, and bounced her head up and down in acknowledgement. "Sweet! See you tomorrow at school, Shell," Hailey chortled and hung up the phone.

Joan moved a step closer and rubbed up and down on Hailey's arm and softly said, " Hey girlfriend, it's been a long day. You're going to have to finish up your calls tomorrow. Let's call it a night."

"Okay Mom," Hailey answered. "I just finished anyway. We're gonna make plans tomorrow at school."

"Alrighty then," Joan concluded, "off with you."

⸙⸙⸙

The next morning when Hailey's mom dropped her off at school, she barely had enough time to wave and say good-bye before her friends descended upon her. Joan stood and watched for a long minute as the girls talked and laughed all at once. "How can they have that much energy?" Joan questioned herself in a low voice that only she could hear, still visualizing the boxes needing to be unpacked at home. Then, she chuckled and added quite happily, "I think I deserve a trip to Starbucks before I get started again." As she drove away, Joan saw the group of girls head in the direction of the classroom. It looked to her like big plans were in the process of being made. "This is going to be a good day," Joan said out loud, "a cinnamon dolce latte with whipped cream good day!"

Hailey and all of her new girlfriends spent every spare second they had that day discussing their plans for the following Saturday. They had all gotten permission from their parents to spend the day at Hailey's house. The girls even decided to invite the boys, Joel, Simon, and Blake, but only because Simon, Rita's brother, knew what was going on. Hailey found out that he had bugged his sister the rest of the night after their phone call.

14

"Yeah," Rita explained, "He was gettin' all up in our business wanting to know what was up."

While listening to Rita, Hailey actually remembered that Blake lived only a few houses away from hers and mentioned it to the rest of the girls. "And if Blake saw us and found out he hadn't been invited," Hailey interjected, "his feelings might really have gotten hurt."

The girls all became quiet and solemn. Hailey could tell that they were thinking about the idea of being left out.

She knew exactly what it felt like to be left out. Being in a wheelchair caused her to be left out of a lot of things.

"Being left out really sucks." Robin finally said, breaking the silence.

The girls grunted in agreement. "Ya know guys, just because they're boys we really shouldn't exclude them. They may be loud and annoying sometimes, but they are still our friends. And besides, we can send them to Blake's house if they get too obnoxious!" Hailey added just before the first bell for class rang.

"To top that off, " Rita piped in, "Simon knows our plan and was asking if he could come." Rita paused and then added, "Just imagine the favor he'll owe me when I tell him *I* worked it out so they all could come."

The girls laughed and slapped a high five over Hailey's head and yelled. "Done!" just as the second bell rang. Hailey watched as everyone gathered their backpacks, put balls and jump ropes back where they belonged, and then hurry toward their classroom.

Mrs. Lacey was waiting at room number eight with the door wide open. She welcomed the children with a "Good morning" as they each entered the classroom. When Mrs. Lacey greeted Hailey, she thought Mrs. Lacey looked like she was super excited today and different than yesterday, the first day of school. When the children had all made it into the classroom and found their seats, Mrs. Lacey took roll, had the class say the pledge of allegiance and then got everyone settled down. It wasn't until then that Hailey noticed the word of the day written on the whiteboard. The word was ANCESTOR. She didn't know what the word meant and couldn't pronounce it as one big word either. She studied the word and tried to sound it out in her head by looking at the different parts of the word, the syllables: An - ces –tor. Hailey uttered the word to herself several times, one syllable at a time, until she could put them all together.

"Humm," she thought, "Ancestor. I think that's right, but I don't know what it means."

"Hey, look," bellowed Joel and pointed to the front of the classroom, "a new word of the day!" The whole class followed the direction of Joel's finger.

"That's right," Mrs. Lacey confirmed.

"Wow," exclaimed Rita, "that looks like a hard one!"

Mrs. Lacey smiled and Hailey could tell that she had a plan. Hailey knew that teachers were sneaky that way. Sometimes they tricked you into learning and sometimes teachers made it a dare. Hailey wondered which one Mrs. Lacey was going to use, the trick or the dare.

"It shouldn't be too hard," Mrs. Lacey goaded. "I heard someone say yesterday's word was too easy. This one isn't any harder; it is just a different one."

"Yeah," Simon agreed. "Yesterday's word was easy because we already knew it, but we didn't know we knew it. We probably already know this one, too." The rest of the class had Simon's back. All of his classmates were bobbing their heads up and down. Hailey watched as each of them looked hard at the new work and attempted to sound it out just like she had a few minutes before.

"Score for Mrs. Lacey. She is going for the dare," Hailey thought to herself, "and it is working." She studied the faces of her classmates and wondered who was going to figure it out first. It didn't look good for Joel and Simon, but Rita and Robin looked like they were close to figuring out the word. Then Hailey saw Robin timidly begin to raise her hand.

"Yes, Robin," Mrs. Lacey responded. "Do you think you know what the word is for today?"

"Yeah, I mean yes, I think I know how to pronounce it, but I don't think I know what it means," Robin replied squirming in her chair.

17

"Well, that's a start," Mrs. Lacey encouraged with a smile. "Tell us what you think the word is and we can work from there."

Hailey heard Robin swallow hard. Robin was probably the shyest and quietest person she knew. She could tell that it was hard for Robin to talk in front of a group of people. Hailey used to be that way, too, afraid to talk in front of people. That was before she had belonged to the Brownies in California where she had been practicing for her Public Speaking Badge. Hailey couldn't wait for the weekend so she could get to know Robin better.

"Well," Robin continued, "I think the word is pronounced 'ancestor'."

Before Mrs. Lacey could even acknowledge Robin's answer, Joel began jumping up and down in his chair and excitedly interjected, "Oh, oh, like that T.V. commercial. Ya know, that one that says 'It all begins with a leaf'. What's it for, aaahhhh, I forget, oh yeah, ancestor.com."

Hailey watched as Mrs. Lacey laughed out loud. She wasn't the only one laughing though. The whole class was laughing at Joel. Hailey didn't think he was trying to be funny and disrupt the class on purpose. She figured that Joel was just that way. He got excited easily and couldn't control it. Joel looked around at his classmates. Hailey could tell that he was puzzled and confused. "What?" he added. "That's what it says."

"Yeah, man, that's right. I've seen that, too. My mom does that on the computer at night after dinner. She looks up different people in our family on that web site and tries to find other people related to us," Simon chimed in. "She said they're all our relatives. Maybe a relative is the same thing as an ancestor."

"Close guys, very close," Mrs. Lacey struggled to get out still laughing," but the commercial is actually for a web site called ancestry.com, and yes an ancestor is a relative but a special kind of relative."

Hailey sat and listened and watched intently as Mrs. Lacey began to draw boxes and lines on the whiteboard and explain what the word ancestor meant. She drew one box and hooked it together with some lines to two more boxes. Then she hooked those boxes with some more line to more boxes. "Wow," Hailey thought to herself, "this looks like it might be kinda hard," but she kept watching and listening. Mrs. Lacey was explaining that a relative is someone in your family. She said that everyone in your family is a relative, but your mom and dad and your grandmother and grandfather are your ancestors. She said the difference between a relative and an ancestor is the word descendant.

"Oh great," Simon blurted out, throwing his hands up in front of himself. "I don't know what that word means either. How am I supposed to figure out a word when the word that helps you figure out the word is another word you don't know?"

Hailey decided that she agreed with Simon. Normally she didn't agree with boys on account of girls were smarter than boys, but today even the girls in her class were mumbling and shaking their heads up and down. It seemed like no one in the whole class understood how they were going to learn the new word...words. "Pretty tricky," Hailey reflected, "turn the word of the day into the words of the day."

"Chill, chill!" Mrs. Lacey coaxed the class. "How about we work this out together. Rita, what do you do when you don't know a word?"

Rita sat quietly for a few seconds. Then she began to rub her forehead and acted like she was thinking and talking at the same time. "Well, I guess I usually ask someone else, like my mom or dad, what a word means."

"Okay," Mrs. Lacey encouraged. "Then what?"

"Oh, oh, I know, I know," Melissa shouted excitedly. "They tell you to look it up! Ya know, like in the dictionary."

"Yes, that is exactly right, Melissa, a dictionary," Mrs. Lacey confirmed. "So, let's get out the dictionary and start to work."

Everyone went to the bookshelf and grabbed a dictionary. Hailey rolled over in her wheelchair and waited until there was room for her to get close enough to get a book down for herself, but before she could get close enough, Blake handed one to her and to Shelly. "I didn't know if you could reach or not. I always help Shelly, so..., anyway." Blake shrugged and walked away like it was no big deal.

"Thanks." Hailey spit over her shoulder as Blake walked back to his desk. By the time Hailey had gotten back to her desk, Mrs. Lacey had written several words on the whiteboard; they were ancestor, relative, and descendant.

"Okay," Mrs. Lacey started, pointing to two rows of desks, "I want you to look up the first word, the second group the second word, and the third group the third word. Then we will share and compare."

Hailey was in the group that had the word 'descendant'. When her group looked it up, they found a couple of definitions. One said *"proceeding from an ancestor or source"*. Another said *"moving or directing downward"*. The group that looked up the word 'ancestor' reported to the class that it meant *"one from whom an individual is descended"*. That was interesting, Hailey thought. Both words had the other word in their definition. The group that had the word 'relative' found that it meant *"a person connected with another by blood or marriage"*. "So," Hailey thought out loud. She really didn't know she said it out loud, but when everyone turned to look at her, she kept going. "So, if Simon and Rita are twins, that makes them

20

relatives because they are brother and sister, right? But they aren't descendants of each other because one didn't come before the other except for maybe a few minutes."

"Yeah," Rita confirmed, I'm two minutes older that Simon."

"Keep going, Hailey," Mrs. Lacey coaxed. "You are going in the right direction."

"Okay," Hailey continued. "Well, you guys know that we just moved here from California. Now we live here in Iowa in my mom's great-grandfather and great-grandmother's house. It's really old, but still kind of cool. And, that means that they were born before my mom and before me. So, I think that means, like the dictionary says, we come from them...we are descending from them. So that would make them my ancestors because they came first and I am their descendant because I came after. Is that right?"

"Terrific!" Mrs. Lacey shouted as she jumped up and down clapping her hands like one of her students.

Shelly shouted out, "You go girl," and joined the rest of the class as they all began clapping, too. Then they laughed when Simon blurted out, "That makes all of them relatives! See, I told you we already knew today's word. In fact, we knew all of today's words."

Simon ran to the front of Hailey's desk and stuck his hand up in the air just above Hailey's head. Hailey didn't hesitate for a second before she slapped his hand in a high five and then ended it with a fist bump.

The weekend could not get here fast enough. Hailey couldn't wait for her friends to start showing up. She had the whole day planned. Hailey and her mom had made snacks for later when they got hungry. They had been to the grocery store that morning and bought juice and fruit. Hailey wished they could have gotten cookies and soda, but when she mentioned it she saw her mom do that thing with her eyebrow...the 'don't go there' eyebrow. The lift had been delivered and installed in the staircase of the basement and Hailey had given it a test ride. It worked PERFECTLY. She would have no problem keeping up with her friends. Hailey could get up and down the basement stairs by herself, and she thought the basement was gonna be a really cool place to make a clubhouse. Even though Hailey and her parents had spent several evenings kind of cleaning it up, the basement still had lots of stuff that Hailey wanted to check out. There was old furniture, boxes, and thing her mom called steamer trunks. She was glad that they had gotten the dirt, dust, cobwebs, and bugs cleaned up. She didn't think the boys would mind the bugs so much, but she didn't like bugs and was pretty sure the other girls wouldn't like them either.

Hailey parked herself at the front door at twelve forty-five, but she couldn't sit still. She spent the next fifteen minutes inching her way up and down the entryway; starting and stopping and spinning little circles with each movement followed by the click of the chair's joystick controller. "Hailey," Joan called from the kitchen. "Stop that clicking. You're driving me a little crazy with that noise. Why don't you just park it for a few minutes?"

"Sorry, Mom," Hailey answered back. "I'm just excited."

"I know sweetie, but that noise is really annoying. It's like fingernails on a chalkboard," Joan returned.

Finally, at one o'clock sharp Hailey's friends started showing up. Robin and her mom were the first to arrive followed by the rest of the girls. Hailey lead the girls down the hall to her bedroom while their moms hung out in the kitchen. "Wow," Melissa gasped, "you really do like purple."

"Yep, I do," Hailey said as she bobbed her head up and down. Then she put her hand on her hip and stuck her nose in the air and continued, "Ya know, purple is the new black, or at least it was in California." All the girls laughed at Hailey. It was a kind of laugh that made her feel good, not bad because they were laughing at her, but laughing at her joke. When the girls finally stopped laughing they heard the voices of the boys. "OMG!" Shelly whispered. "They're actually here. They really came. I didn't think they would want to hang out with us girls."

"Why wouldn't they," Hailey questioned and then added," and we did promise food, remember?" Once again the girls laughed.

Hailey's mom hollered down the hall. "Hailey, the rest of your guests are here."

"Okay, Mom, we're coming," Hailey squealed. The girls headed back down the hallway to the kitchen. They all said 'Hi' to the boys and 'Goodbye' to their moms.

"So, what are we gonna do now?" asked Joel.

"Well," Hailey said, "I have a plan. We have this basement ..."

"So," Joel interrupted, "we all have basements."

"I know, may I finish, please?" Hailey countered. "We have this basement and there are lots of boxes, and trunks, and old, old furniture, and just stuff down there. My dad says that no one really knows what's in them, the boxes and trunks, 'cause no one ever bothered to check it out after my grandma J.J. died. Her name was really Juanita Josephine, but we called her J.J. So," Hailey continued staring straight at Joel, "I thought it would be cool to make like a clubhouse down there and pretend the boxes and stuff hold like secret clues to something."

"Wow, you came up with a good idea for a girl," Simon stated. Rita reached over and punched Simon in the arm. "Hey," Simon whined, "I said it was a good idea, Rita, why did you hit me." Rita turned and faced the group of girls

23

while she placed her index finger by the side of her head and made small circles. The girls giggled, mostly because they thought it was funny when the twins fought.

"Okay, so let's go," Blake coaxed. "I want to see what's down there. We just use our basement for storms. There isn't anything cool or mysterious or secret in ours."

Hailey lead her group of friends to the outside door where the basement opened up into the backyard. None of

her friends had ever seen or used a wheelchair lift before, so Hailey had to explain to them how it helped her get up and down the stairs. She showed them how she got into the closed-in platform, closed the door, and pushed the down button. Hailey rode the lift down and then sent it back up to the top of the stairs so her friends could ride it down, too.

"That is way cool," Joel praised. "I wish we had one of these in our basement or even in our house. I would never have to walk up or down the stairs again." Once again all of the friends laughed at Joel. Hailey knew that he really didn't mean to be funny. It was just the way he was…funny. They all stopped laughing when Hailey turned on the lights and they could see what was waiting for them in the basement of Hailey's great- great-grandmother's house.

"Wow!" they all exclaimed while looking around at all of the stuff.

"This is like, way cool," Robin added. "It's like a maze made of boxes and trunks, and look, there's one of those things you put clothes on, what do you call it, oh yeah, a mannequin.

"I told you guys that there was all kinds of stuff down here," Hailey boasted. "My mom, and I already kind of cleared out a space over there, see?" Hailey pointed toward the middle of the room. "Then my mom and dad set up some of the chairs and tables for us 'cause they thought they might be too heavy for us to move."

Joel, Blake, and Simon all looked at each other and tried to pump up big muscles in their arms. "We could've done it, no problem," Simon spoke for the boys.

The girls laughed and in unison held up their hands in front of the boys and said, "Whatever!"

Hailey could tell that the boys were feeling a little deflated. She so knew what it felt like to have someone tell you that you couldn't do something. People told her that all the time and it sucked. Just because she was in a wheelchair didn't mean that she was incapable of doing anything. She could do a lot of stuff. She decided the best thing to do was to ask the boys to move some of the boxes over to the tables so they could look through them. "That," Hailey thought, "would make them feel better."

"So guys, how about bringing some of the boxes over here," Hailey politely asked the boys, pointing to the table.

26

The boys puffed out their chests and strutted over to one of the boxes. It took all three of them to lift it and get it to the table, but they got it there. "See," Joel defended, "we can do it." The other two boys proudly shook their heads up and down in agreement.

The friends spent the next several hours exploring the basement and going through many of the boxes and trunks. They found clothes that looked really old. The boys didn't care too much about the clothes, but the girls thought they were kind of cool but kind of weird at the same time. They were really big and sort of fluffy. They found old dishes, and fancy silverware, and jewelry, and tools, knickknacks, and baby clothes. Then Shelly and Rita drug a big steamer trunk out from the corner of the basement. "Hey, guys, check this out," Shelly called. She had opened the trunk and found bunches of pictures, some old pamphlets about Iowa, and a shoebox full of letters. All of the children crowded around Shelly who was holding the shoebox. The first things she pulled out were three really old postcards.

"Wow," Blake exclaimed, "check out the dates on these. They say 1942, and they were mailed from Des Moines, Iowa to someplace called Scotch Grove, Iowa."

"But look," Robin noticed, "there isn't any address, I mean, look, no house number, or street, or even a zip code. How weird is that and how did they get to where they were supposed to go?" Robin questioned.

That is weird, Hailey thought. She was new to Iowa, but she knew that you had to have a whole address to mail something to somebody no matter where you lived, even in Iowa. "Let me see those for a second," Hailey said as she reached out for the post cards. She began to read the first card to everyone.

We are still at Camp Dodge. We took tests today and will get our uniforms tomorrow. It was cloudy all day down here, a swell day to start the army. I may not write now for a few days because I don't know where I'll go. We will probably leave here tomorrow nite. so I'll send my clothes home tomorrow. But I'll keep my shoes as I can keep brown for off duty.

Maynard

"Hummmm," Hailey thought out loud. "Maynard is his first name and I think Kuhns would've been his last name on account of that's who it was mailed to, and he's talking about sending his clothes home, like to his mom or something. No, wait a sec," she corrected herself as she flipped the post card over, "this is addressed to someone named Harry H. Kuhns. That isn't his mom, maybe it's his dad." Hailey intently studied the postcards for several minutes while her friends waited patiently. "Oh, oh, I know who this is ... or was..." Hailey reflected. "It's Maynard Kuhns. He's my great- grandpa, but he died." She looked up and smiled at her friends. "So if Harry was Maynard's dad that would make him my great-great-grandpa and like we learned in school, they are my ancestors. This is too cool; I have postcards and letters written by my ancestors."

Rita agreed, "Yeah, this is way cool, this postcard is seventy years old. And look, they spelled things different then." The rest of the group looked over Hailey's shoulder at the postcard trying to figure out what Rita was talking about. "Look," Rita pointed, "we don't spell 'night' like that."

"That is kinda different," Joel confirmed. "But where is Camp Dodge and why is he sending his clothes home?" They all gave Joel a vacant stare. Hailey knew he was used to getting looks like that. He always asked off the wall questions or just said really odd things. That's what makes Joel, Joel, she thought to herself, smiling and shaking her head.

"Well, if you look, JOEL, it says that he's starting the army. Then if you read the next postcard, it says that he got

28

his uniform, and that he had bunches of test and shots," Robin pointed out as she flipped to the third card. "This one says that he's leaving to go train for the army and that army life is 'OK'." Robin looked up to see all of her friends with a blank expression on their faces.

Okay, maybe I judged Joel fast, Hailey admitted to herself and asked the question she knew they all wanted an answer to, "So, where did Maynard go to train for the army?"

"Yeah," they all chimed in, "Where did he go?"

"Hey kids," Hailey's dad said as he came down the basement stairwell. "How's it going? You have been down here for hours. I was beginning to think that you were all buried alive under all of this stuff." Then Andrew looked around the room approvingly and nodded his head and added, "Wow, you guys have been really busy. It actually looks organized down here. I may have to hire the bunch of you for my office at work. I still have boxes that need to be unpacked."

Hailey and her friends laughed. They had spent the last four hours having the best time ever, exploring and arranging things, that they didn't even realize they had been working so hard. Hailey even realized that she and the girls hadn't even once threatened to send the boys to Blake's house for being obnoxious.

"No thanks, Mr. Burke, it'd probably cost you too much to hire all of us." Simon spoke for the group.

"I suppose so," Hailey's dad mused, "but the real reason I came down was to tell you that your parents are here to pick you up, except for Blake. Your mom called to see when you were coming home. She said since you live a couple of doors down, you could walk." That made Blake make a pouty face while the other children pointed their fingers and laughed at him. Hailey knew that she and her friends weren't making fun of him; they were just teasing him a little.

"That's okay," Blake playfully retorted. "That just means that I live close enough that I can come back anytime I want and help Hailey go through the rest of the letters and stuff, so humph."

"No fair," Rita sounded off.

"Hey, guys," Hailey broke in before Rita could start an all-out boy girl war, "let's ask my dad about Maynard's postcards before you have to go home."

"Postcards, Maynard, what are you kids talking about?" Andrew asked.

Hailey explained to her dad how she and her friends had spent the entire afternoon cleaning and setting up a clubhouse. The rest of the children remained silent while she told him how they started going through some of the boxes and found all sorts of old things, really old things. Then she picked up the shoebox full of letters and handed it to her dad along with the three postcards Robin had been reading. "Then we found these," She stated. "I think these are all from my Great-Grandpa Maynard, ya know, Mom's grandpa, to his parents."

"Wow," Andrew exclaimed, rifling through the letters. "That is some impressive detective work. They have to be over, what, fifty years old."

"More like seventy, Mr. Burke," Rita corrected.

"Yeah, but look at this postcard," Hailey said holding it up to her dad. "There isn't a real address on it. The *who* it's from address is missing and the *who* it's to address doesn't have enough. Then look at the letters. The *who* it's from address has way too much to be an address."

Andrew looked at the postcard and chuckled out loud. He could see right away why the children were

30

confused. "I see your dilemma," he acknowledged. "I think we have a couple of minutes for me to explain this." Winking at the group, Andrew continued. "You know moms; they'll be up in the kitchen talking forever anyway."

All of the children, along with Andrew, moved over to the couch and chairs that they had set up earlier around the tables. Hailey rolled her wheelchair into the spot that purposely was left open for her. Andrew laid the cards and letters on the table, cleared his throat and began. "Okay, class, this is our first lesson on the United States Postal Service."

"Dad," Hailey shouted as the rest of the children laughed, "Be serious!"

"Okay, okay," Andrew answered throwing his hands up in front of his face. "Serious...I got it." He picked up all three cards and read what was written on each one. Then he flipped them over and studied the front of the postcards, where the address was supposed to be.

Hailey and her friends sat pensively as they waited for Andrew to finish examining the cards and letters. Then she watched her Dad go into his pondering mode, the one where he put his thumb and his finger on his chin looking up at the ceiling. While they waited, Hailey looked around at her friends and noticed that Joel was even sitting quietly, patiently waiting for her Dad. He must really be interested in this, Hailey thought to herself. This is so not like him. She was sure he had ADHD or something. Ever since the first day they met he was like a worm just wiggling all the time. Hailey was startled out of her thoughts when her dad started talking.

"Well," he began. "First off, the return address on any piece of mail isn't really needed, isn't necessary unless you want something returned to you or mailed to you at that address. Like in case the person you are sending it to doesn't have your address. But look here," Andrew said as he pointed at the first postcard, the one dated September 3, 1942.

All of the children looked at what Andrew was showing them. Hailey read the first few lines of the card to herself until she got to the line that read:

I may not write now for a few days because I don't know where I'll go. We will probably leave here tomorrow...

"Oh, I get it," she chirped.

"Yeah, me too," Robin agreed. "Maynard didn't put a who it's from address, I mean a return address, because he isn't going to be living at Camp Dodge, where ever that is, on account of he's leaving there in a couple of days," she added as she grabbed for the postcard dated September 5, 1942. "See," she pointed out as she read the card.

"...we just got out orders to leave for our camps for basic training."

"Well, that makes sense, I guess," Joel mumbled scratching his head while he threw his feet up on the table.

"Dude, get your feet of the table," Rita scolded. "How rude, and besides that your feet stink."

Joel slowly pulled his feet off of the table and folded his arms over his chest, slumping back in the chair. "Sorry," he whispered. Then even quieter he added, "And my feet do not stink."

Hailey could tell that Joel was embarrassed and she felt a little sorry for him. She didn't feel sorry for him because he got yelled at. That happened all the time. She felt sorrier for him because it happened in front of her dad, a grownup. Hailey watched Joel's face turn super red and his ears turn pink. She had never seen anyone turn that color before. "Jeez," she thought, "I hope he doesn't start crying.

That would be really embarrassing for him." She didn't know what to do so she looked to her dad for some kind of help. Andrew understood right away by the look in her eye what Hailey was thinking and silently asking. It only took him a second to get the children's attention back on the postcards and off of Joel.

"Let's look at the addressee on this," Andrew quickly said.

Hailey blew out a big breath and mouthed the words 'Thank You' to her dad. The rest of her friends looked at Hailey's dad too, but for a different reason. At exactly the same time the all exclaimed, "The what?"

"The addressee," Andrew repeated. "What you guys were calling the "*who it's to address.*"

"Yeah," Melissa added shrugging her shoulders. "I don't get that at all. It's weird. How did any of these cards and letters get to where they were supposed to? They only had someone's name and the words *Scotch Grove, Iowa* on them," she continued to explain after she pulled more letters out of the shoe box and spread them out on the table.

After studying the envelopes on the table, Hailey and her friends agreed with Melissa, and Simon actually said it. "It is weird. I mean, I know mine and Rita's address is 1492 Willow Drive, Monticello, Iowa, 52310, and you gotta put it all on the envelope if you want to mail it...and someone to get it."

"You are absolutely right," Andrew agreed. "But that's now in the twenty-first century and you live in the big city of Monticello. Scotch Grove is a whole lot smaller. Wait a second," he added. "Didn't I see some books or pamphlets on Iowa that you found?"

"Yeah, they're right here," Shelly said pushing some of the stuff on the table out of the way. "I put 'em here so we could look at them later."

"Great, let's see if they will help me explain," Andrew said, reaching for them.

33

He flipped through the pages and read for what seemed like a bazillion years to Hailey. She was glad when he finally looked up, took a big breath and started talking. He began by telling Hailey and her friends that people first came to Scotch Grove in about 1836. The people were from Scotland, and that is probably where the name came from. Those people had left Scotland because life was hard and they wanted to try someplace they thought might be better, and after a really long time and thousands of miles they found themselves in a place that is called the state of Iowa today. They first called it a settlement of Scotch Grove Township. That's because Iowa wasn't even a state yet. It was what was called a territory. Iowa didn't become a state until 1846.

"Mr. Burke," Blake interrupted. "That's all kind of interesting, but I don't understand. What is a township and what does all of this have to do with the address?"

"Yeah Dad," Hailey agreed rolling her arm in front of herself signaling her dad to hurry up.

"Sorry honey, you know how I get all involved and sidetracked," Andrew apologized.

"That's okay," Melissa commented, giggling through her fingers covering her mouth. "My dad does the same thing. He always wants us to learn stuff and I guess we do just by listening." All of the children laughed and shook their heads up and down in agreement. Hailey caught Joel mimicking someone talking a lot by putting his hand in front of his mouth and opened and closed his fingers really fast. He stopped and sat on his hands when Rita gave him a 'behave yourself in front of adults' kind of look. Joel stuck his chin out and gave Rita the 'I didn't do anything" look and stuck his tongue out at her.

"Thanks, Melissa, I appreciate that." Andrew answered with a smile as he set down the book. "Let's see if I can get to the point." Andrew began to explain to the children what he had just read in the booklet. He started by telling them that Scotch Grove is actually about seven miles from Monticello, where they all live now. Then he explained that a township is a chunk of land that is six miles by six miles; like a big block or square of land. Sometimes there is a town in that space and sometimes it's just farm land with a family running, working and living on the farm. He went on to explain that most farms back then, in 1942, were around 120 acres. "So," Andrew challenged, let's do the math. Shelly, I hear you are good at math. Help me out here."

Shelly beamed as she answered Hailey's dad, "Okay, give it to me."

Andrew handed Shelly the mechanical pencil he always carried in his shirt pocket along with the little notebook. "Here is the information you need to figure out what we need to know. We know that a township is six by six miles. If you multiple those numbers you get square miles. I am going to tell you that there are 640 acres in one square mile, and remember that we talked about farms back then were about 120 acres."

All of the children were paying close attention to Andrew. Even though math wasn't usually very fun or exciting for any of them, except Shelly, they were all stoked about figuring out the answer, or at least having Shelly figure it out.

Shelly wrote in the notebook the numbers Andrew had given her. *Six, six, 640, and 120.* Then she wrote down by the numbers: *multiply, square mile, family, farm, and acres.* She stared at the numbers and words for a few seconds.

"She is really thinking hard on this one," Hailey thought to herself. She knew that six times six equaled 36, but math wasn't her thing so she wasn't sure what to do with that. "Maybe that's a square mile," she guessed.

"Come on, Shelly," Simon coaxed leaning forward.

Hailey reached her arm across Simon's chest pushing him back in his seat when Shelly looked up and gave him a look like she wanted to sock him in the face. At the same time Rita motioned with her finger over her mouth and a long "Ssshhhhhh," for her twin brother to keep quiet.

"Okay, okay," he responded.

It only took Shelly a few minutes to figure out what to do with the numbers. She just wasn't sure what the answer represented. The final number she came up with was 192. When she was done checking to make sure her answer was right, she pushed the notebook over to Andrew. "So, the answer is 192, but 192 what?" she asked.

"I want you all to think for a second," Andrew said. "What did we want to know in the beginning?" When he got only blank looks from his young students, he added and pushed the notebook back to the center of the table. "What word doesn't have a number to go along with it?"

They group studied the notebook. They all compared the numbers and words Shelly had written down to do her calculations. Hailey noticed that the words family and farm were the two words that didn't have a number to go with them. Just as she was ready to answer her dad's question, Joel blurted out, "OH, OH, I think I know. I think the number 192 is the number of farms and families on the farms in that place....ya know that place we've been talking about."

All at once the children yelled, "Scotch Grove!"

"Yep, that's the place," Joel proudly answered. "Scotch Grove."

"Good job, Joel, Shelly, and everyone else," Andrew praised, and held his hand up before Hailey could finish the question she had started to ask. "Just think a second, Shelly and Joel have figured out that there were 192 farms and families in the six by six mile area of Scotch Grove Township, Right?" The children all mumbled a yes and Andrew continued. "So, what I'm getting at with all of this is that if there were only 192 families living in a place, the mailman probably knew everyone and their names and their children. Once the mail got to Scotch Grove, which is on the postcards and letters you guys found, he probably knew who H. H. Kuhns or even Mrs. H. H. Kuhns was and which farm they lived on." Andrew explained.

"What!?" Simon blasted.

"It's like, how many third grade classrooms are there at your school," Andrew prompted the group.

Robin was the first to answer. "Six and they are all in building D."

"Perfect example," Andrew coached, "that would be your third grade township and I bet you know everyone in those six rooms."

"Well, yeah, of course," Joel spouted.

"Well, there you go. If you were the third grade township's mailman you would know exactly who got what mail," Andrew concluded.

"I think I want to be a mailman when I grow up," Joel announced. "On account-a I bet I know almost everybody in t-h-e w-o-r-l-d," he added, jumping up off of the couch holding his arms up in the air opened wide apart.

Everyone, even Andrew, burst into a fit of laughter. That was just like Joel, Hailey thought as she laughed so hard she started crying; thinking he knows everything, and everyone. She figured that he must do that because of his big brother, Aaron who was in high school. Joel had told her that Aaron was kind of really smart, had lots of friends, had a job, had taken a trip last summer with some of his friends cross country to visit other friends, and was on some sports team at school. Since Hailey wasn't very interested in sports she kind of didn't remember what sports Aaron played, but it seemed super important to Joel. She guessed that Joel wanted to be just like his big brother.

Joan had been standing at the top of the stairs of the basement for several minutes observing her husband with the group of children. She had tried to call down to them but couldn't be heard because of all of the laughing going on. When the laughter had subsided, Joan tried again. "Hey," she yelled and had a room full of shocked faces looking up at her. "Are you guys alive down there or did a box fall on the group of you? I've got some moms up here that have been waiting for *someone* to bring a group of kids up from the basement. "

Andrew turned toward the group and mouthed the word "Busted".

Hailey muffled a giggle and answered her mom. "We're all okay, Mom. Dad was just explaining something to us."

"Say no more," Joan surrendered holding her hands up in front of her face. Hailey could see that her mom was pretending to be mad, but really wasn't because you don't smile when you're mad. "We all know what happens when Dad starts explaining something…it never ends."

All of the children tried to stifle their laughs as they started toward the stairs and lift. They all knew it wasn't nice to laugh at people, but it was hard not to laugh at Hailey's parents right now because they were making fun of each other in a fun way, not a mean way.

Simon startled the group to a stop when he bellowed, "Wait!" When they had all turned around to face Simon, he went on, "What about the big address on the envelopes? You didn't tell us about that one yet."

"Hey, buddy," Andrew gently responded. "We'll have to do that another time. We ran out of time today." Waving his arm in a huge ark, Andrew joked. "All this stuff isn't going anywhere. It will all be here next time you come over."

Before Simon could protest, Hailey's mom began singing the song from the movie *Madagascar,* "…you've got to move it, move it, move it…"

That night after her friends had left and her family had eaten dinner, Hailey asked for permission to use the computer. She wanted to try and look up the big return address that was on the envelopes in the box full of letters. She wanted to surprise Simon on Monday with what she could find out. After searching for some time, Hailey found what she was looking for. First, she had to figure out that what she thought was a 2 in the third line was actually a Q. After she did that she found out that Q M Repl Tng Center was an abbreviation for Quartermaster Replacement Training Center that was started in February of 1941, at a place called Camp Lee in the state of Virginia. Hailey read on and learned that the Quartermaster Corp is one of three U.S. Army logistics (whatever logistic meant, she'd have to look that word up later) branches, the other two are the Transportation Corps and the Ordnance Corps. "Way too much information," Hailey commented to herself as she continued reading. *This school provides soldiers with special training, something called advanced individual training or AIT and leader training for Quartermaster officers, warrant officers and non-commissioned officers.* "Again," Hailey groaned. Simon might want to know this stuff, but she definitely didn't. She would remember to give him the web address to read about all of this himself. She just wanted to know where the heck her great-grandfather was when he went into the army. After reading for several more minutes, Hailey decided that Quartermaster training was a school or a place where army guys could learn some kind of special job that they would work while in the army. She found a list of some of the things, special jobs, she guessed, that her great-grandpa might have gone to school to learn. She read through the list, but didn't really understand what they were, except maybe the one that said food service operations or the one that said laundry and clothing repair specialist. She figured that one had something to do with sewing, like fixing rips in clothes or putting buttons back on shirts that were lost.

Hailey stopped reading and looked at the clock in the lower right hand side of the computer. It was already three minutes after nine o'clock. She knew her mom would be coming to tell her that it was time for bed soon. She glanced back up at the computer screen and scrolled through the rest of the list of jobs. "Blah, blah, blah, blah," Hailey chanted as she rocked her head back and forth. "Lists are way boring. I'm going to bed."

The next day was Sunday. Hailey still had a little bit of homework to finish before Monday. She got up, got dressed, and hurried into the kitchen for breakfast. Her plan was to spend some more time in the basement today

40

checking out more of the letters she and her friends had found on Saturday. She would do that after she finished her homework, she promised herself. As she rolled into the kitchen her mom looked up from the newspaper and smiled. "Good morning, Sunshine. What's your plan for today?"

Hailey wheeled over to the counter and got a bowl, a spoon, and the box of her favorite cereal. She looked in the refrigerator for the milk only to discover that it was already on the table. "Well," she began while she poured herself a big bowl of cereal, "I thought I would go back downstairs and do some more investigating. Ya know that box of letters we found?" Hailey didn't wait for an answer but continued using her spoon as a pointer. "We only got to read the first three postcards. I want to read some more. We're learning about ancestors and descendants and like that at school and I thought it would be cool if I could find out more about Great-Grandpa Maynard and maybe share it at school."

"And homework?" Joan questioned with a raised eyebrow.

Man, Hailey thought. How does she do that? She always knows when I haven't done all of my homework. "Oh, yeah," Hailey waved her spoon in response. " I'm gonna take it down with me and do it first before I start checking out other stuff."

"Alright, just making sure," Joan replied with a wink. "Maybe later you might want to go help me get a feel for how my new shop should look."

"Sure," Hailey answered as she scarfed down the rest of her breakfast and then headed out the door and onto the lift that took her down to the basement...the clubhouse that still needed a name. "Hummm, a name," Hailey thought out loud. "Maybe one of the other kids had come up with a good name."

Hailey did as she had promised her mom. She scooted up to the table with her school books and finished her homework first. When that was done she grabbed the shoebox and pulled out a handful of letters and started reading them one by one. The first one after the postcards was dated September 8, 1942. By reading it, Hailey found out that her great-grandpa was four or five hundred miles from home and that he had been through Illinois, Indiana, Ohio, and West Virginia to get to Virginia where Camp Lee was located. This letter also had his new address and explained what it meant. "Simon is gonna like this," Hailey said to herself. She would make sure to show it to him.

Pvt Maynard Kuhns
Co. M. 7th QM Regt.
Camp Lee, VA.

That means:

Company M 7th
Quarter Master Replacement Training Center.

On Monday morning Hailey was excited for more than one reason. First, she liked school and was ready to go back and see her friends. She couldn't wait to share with them all of the facts and information she had found on the computer Saturday night. The second reason she was excited was because her mom didn't have to drive her to school in their handicapped accessible van anymore. The school had *finally* received the school bus that had a ramp and tie downs, just like her mom's van. That made the school bus *totally* accessible for her and her wheelchair. Now she could ride to school like the other kids, with the other kids.

Hailey thought she might have been nervous riding the bus, but she wasn't scared at all because Blake said that he would sit in one of the regular seats next to her and introduce her to the other kids that lived on their block that would be riding the bus, too.

Hailey looked at the clock on her nightstand just as her mother called for her to come to breakfast. "I'll be right there," she answered. "I just gotta make sure I've got all my homework and stuff." Hailey realized that she probably needed to hurry because the bus was supposed to pick her up at seven-thirty and it was already five minutes after seven. That was one bad thing about riding the bus. She had to get up earlier and be ready sooner.

Hailey made it to the kitchen in time to shovel down a bowl of cinnamon apple oatmeal and a glass of milk before she hugged her mom and was out on the front porch waiting for the bus at seven-twenty-five. "Score!" Hailey breathed as she pumped her arm up and down. "Five minutes to spare. Am I good or what?"

Hailey heard her mom laugh and turned to see her standing in the doorway. "Mom!" She scolded. "What are you doing? I can do this by myself."

"I know honey," Joan replied. "I'm sorry…" Before she could finish her sentence, Joan noticed someone running down the sidewalk toward her and Hailey. Pointing, Joan said, "Look."

Hailey spun her chair around to face where her mom was pointing and saw Blake running down the sidewalk. "Hey, Blake, What are you doin'," Hailey hollered through her hands tunneled around her mouth.

It was several seconds before Blake made it to Hailey's porch and a couple more before he could catch his breath to answer. "I'm riding the bus to school with you, remember?" he puffed out.

"Oh, yeah, I know but I thought you were getting on at your house," Hailey questioned.

"Well, yeah, I was gonna get on at my house, but I asked my mom if I could come down to your house to help you get on the bus." Blake paused and added, "Only if you need it though."

Hailey's mom stepped back inside the front door to leave her daughter and her friend to wait for the bus together. Just before she closed the door, Joan heard Hailey's response. "Cool. Thanks, Blake. Actually, I don't know if the new bus driver knows how to tie down wheelchairs. He might need help."

"How come your mom is laughing?" Blake asked when he heard Joan behind the door.

Hailey listened for a second and commented. "I don't know. Parents are just weird sometimes."

"Yeah, I know," Blake agreed.

All week long Hailey and her friends talked and planned for their next day exploring in Hailey's basement. During that time they had finally agreed on a name for their club. One day at recess, Melissa brought her dictionary out onto the playground. She had bookmarked some words she thought might work for a club name. She explained that she had looked up words like basement, underground, and even a new one she had learned, catacomb. "Check it out," Melissa urged while she held the book open. "They all have the word "secret" in the definition. So, I was thinkin', since there are seven of us, we could call the club *Secret Seven Catacomb Hunters.*"

"Yeah, that would be a super cool name!" Joel and Simon agreed simultaneously.

Joel continued, "That's perfect 'cause the basement is underground and we're finding all kinds of hidden or forgotten things in all those boxes and trunks. And," Joel added, "no one will know what we found, unless we want them to know. But wait a second," he added a quickly. "There are eight of us. I think you forgot someone."

"Man, me and my numbers, again," Melissa groaned. "I think I forgot myself. Oops. Now that name won't work."

"But I have one that will," Hailey said. "How about *Super Secret Catacomb Hunters?*"

Joel looked at Hailey with a big grin on his face. "I like it."

When Saturday finally arrived, Hailey could hardly wait for her friends to show up. Once again she, not-so-patiently, sat at the window next to the front door watching. She saw Robin's mom's car pull up in front of her house. Robin got out and waved to her mom as the car drove away. Hailey was at the front door and rolling onto the porch before Robin could even knock. The girls greeted each other with a giant hug and headed to the side of the house where the basement door and lift were located. The two of them got on the lift and went down together chattering the whole way. It wasn't long before the rest of the group were also making their way to the *Super Secret Catacomb Hunter's* headquarters, better known as the *SSCH* headquarters, located in Hailey Burke's family basement via the wheelchair lift.

"Yo," Joel yelled when the lift stopped. "How long you guys been down here? I thought we were meeting at noon. You haven't started reading the letters yet, have you?"

"Chill out dude," Hailey tried to soothe. "Robin just got here like five minutes ago and we haven't even had time to do anything. Besides, we wouldn't start without you."

"Okay, good, I was just worried I might'a missed something," Joel answered as he plopped on the couch next to Robin. "Let's get this started then."

It wasn't long before all of the children had arrived and were reaching into the box of letters that had been left in the middle of the table. Each one grabbed a handful and settled back on the couch, or in the piles of blankets and pillows, to read their bunch of letters.

"Remember," Hailey prompted, "If you guys find something cool or interesting, or weird, or whatever, you need to read it out loud."

"Got it," Rita acknowledged for the group. "We want to find out about Maynard Kuhns and the rest of Hailey's ancestors and their history and like that."

"Exactly!" Hailey agreed.

The children read to themselves for several minutes, lost in the pages of the life of Hailey's great-grandpa Maynard. The first one to speak was Simon. "Hey guys, listen to this. He isn't at Camp Lee any more. He's some place called Baltimore, and he got to see Washington D.C., too." All of the children remained quiet while Simon read the letter to them.

Dear Folks,

Well here goes for a letter from Baltimore. We got here last night but I didn't have time to write to you before in fact I haven't even written to Helen.

46

Well this camp is a Motor Ordinance Base and the school is very much like I had before. But the camp is very much nice. It is right in Baltimore or rather on the edge. It is a much smaller camp and it doesn't seem so much like being penned in as it did down in Lee. And the air it is just like home nice & fresh.

We came through Washington D.C. and I got to see the Capital. Only I didn't get to see enough of it. The towns around there really suffered from the flood. A lot of bridges were washed out. I hope you didn't have that much rain around home.

I'm going to try and get in the Air Corps after I get done here. But I don't know how it will work. But at least I can try. We are studying carburetors and electricity now & will for 2 weeks...They really have the food here. And all and everything you want. I sure hope I don't have to go across from here. But if I have to go across I don't suppose it will be so nice.

Your Son,

Maynard
10/20/42
Holobird Ordinance Motor Base
5th Prov. Co.
Baltimore, Maryland

"Wow," Shelly commented. "He was kind of a long way from home, and he got to see the Capital and everything. I wonder what it means to 'go over', and what flood do you think he was talking about?"

Blake thought out loud. "Do we have a secretary or something? We should write down or make a list of all the things we have questions about. Then we can ask someone like Mrs. Lacey or Mr. Burke about them."

"Good idea," they all answered.

Simon took it one step further and asked, "Do we need officers, ya know, like president, vice-president, treasurer, secretary and like that?"

The rest of the group looked blankly at Simon. Then they looked at each other, shrugged their shoulders and discussed the idea of needing officers for their eight member club. It was decided that they didn't need a treasurer because they didn't have any money to keep track of anyway. The girls pretty much decided that they didn't want the boys to think they were in charge, and the boys didn't want the girls to think they were in charge, so they all decided that they really didn't need or want a president or vice- president either. The only thing they really needed was someone to write down the questions they wanted to ask an adult about, the stuff they didn't know or understand in the letters. At first, no one stepped up to take the job. Hailey figured it probably sounded too much like homework or something to her friends. It did kind of sound like that to her, too, but she thought that if they were going to remember what they wanted to ask then they should probably write it down.

Hailey knew that Melissa had trouble with her letters and numbers sometimes. She got them mixed up and backwards. Hailey's mom always told her that if someone had a hard time with something they should practice it until it wasn't so hard. Unlike Shelly, Hailey hated math and wasn't very good at it, so she practiced to get better. She did have the prime numbers memorized because her dad helped her all the time. And that gave Hailey an idea. She told the group that she would write down the questions they came up with if Melissa would help her.

Melissa looked surprised and almost embarrassed by Hailey's suggestion. "I don't think so, Hailey," Melissa stammered. "You know I have issues…"

48

"Ah, come on. How are you going to get better if you don't practice and just do it?" Hailey coaxed. "And besides, I'm gonna help you."

"But it might take me a long time," Melissa persisted.

"You don't think it takes me twice as long to do stuff that you can do super-fast?" Hailey pointed out.

"Yeah," the rest of the children protested.

Robin added, "We all have things we can't do as good or as fast as somebody else. Look at Joel and me. He makes friends fast and talks all the time, and I would never talk to people I don't know."

'That's 'cause you're shy and I'm not," Joel clarified.

"Alright," Melissa surrendered. "I'll do it on two conditions: First, Hailey, you have to help me, and second, you guys have to stop sounding like my mom."

"Okay, done," Hailey answered for the whole group as she looked around the room bobbing her head up and down, attempting to get the rest of her friends to do the same.

Hailey watched as Robin jumped up and went to her backpack and pulled out a small pink binder and a pencil. Hailey knew she only used this binder for very important things, things like songs and people's phone numbers and e-mail addresses. She offered it to Melissa to use until they were able to get another one just for the *SSCH Club.*

"Alright then, let's make a list," Melissa said taking the notepad and pencil.

Over the next hour the group re-read the letter several times and each one made suggestions on what questions should go on the list. Melissa had scooted up to the table with Hailey so they could concentrate on what they were writing and not on trying to balance the notebook on one of their laps. Melissa looked a little nervous to Hailey, so she whispered, "It's okay, I'm gonna help, remember, and when we get our club binder or whatever, we can copy it over to make sure there are no mistakes. This will be like our rough draft, ya know, like we always do when we write something at school."

Melissa nodded in agreement and held the pencil over the blank page. "Okay, mark, set, go," she uttered with more confidence.

Shelly's questions were the first on the list. One was *'what does go across mean'* and *'what flood was Maynard talking about'* was the second. Joel wanted to know *'what the Air Corps was'*, so that was the third.

"Hey, guys, we probably should have read these in order. Maybe we can just put our questions in order so they make more sense," Robin suggested.

They agreed on putting the letters in order of their dates. The very first two, the postcards, had the same date, September 3, 1942. When they looked closer at the letters, the group found out that they also had a time stamped on them. After trying to decide if that was important, Joel offered Shelly to put the letters and cards in time order, too. "Since you are good at math and numbers and stuff, I figured you'd be the best one to do it," Joel said to justify his idea.

Shelly scrunched her eyebrows together and stared at Joel. "Why don't you do it?"

"'Cause I'm not good at that and you are, duhh," Joel answered holding his hands up and shrugging his shoulders.

Hailey jumped in to stop the two from getting into an argument. She suggested that maybe they could put the letters in order together. She explained that just like Melissa, he wasn't going to get any better at math and numbers if he didn't do math and numbers. Shelly agreed that that would be a good idea, and Joel didn't believe that it would work, that he would learn math better, but he said he would help Shelly.

So, the whole group started putting the letters they had already read in piles by month. Then Shelly and Joel took them and arranged them by date and time on the envelopes. The children figured out that Maynard sent a letter almost every day. Sometimes he sent more than one in a day, so Joel thought that knowing what time they were sent was good to know, too. He wasn't sure yet why, but he was sure Shelly would come up with some reason. They had read letters from part of the months of September, October, and November. The group found out that by reading handfuls of letters, all hodge-podge like they had done, they had missed some of the letters altogether. Rita suggested that they start over and read them in the order that Shelly and Joel were putting them. "Yeah," Simon agreed. "We can take turns reading them so we don't get tired."

Rita shook her head and just said, "Boys."

"Yeah, but it's a good idea," defended Blake. "Even your mouth has got to get tired after a while."

51

All of the boys laughed at what Blake had said, even though he was being serious. Even Hailey and the other girls giggled a little bit. Rita's face turned bright red and she turned and slugged her brother, Simon, in the arm.

"Ouch, why did you hit me? I didn't say it, Blake said it." Simon complained.

"Because you laughed," Rita grumbled. "And besides I can't hit Blake 'cause he's my friend."

Simon looked at his sister, scratched his head and said. "Whatever…"

Shelly and Joel had been working on the month of September and had gotten the whole month in order. While they started working on October, Blake began reading the first letter after the postcards. He read through about ten letters. Some of them he had read before, but some he had not. As he was reading, when anyone had a question about something in the letters, Melissa and Hailey would make a note of it in the binder. Some of the letters were interesting, some were funny, some they didn't understand, and some were kind of boring.

"Man, this is gonna take forever doing it this way," Joel complained, fidgeting in his seat.

The next one to read was Rita. She looked at Joel and Joel knew he had better be quiet. He was her friend too, but she had punched him before so he knew she would do it again. When Joel had settled back down, Rita read another ten letters.

Simon volunteered to read next. He read five letters out loud and then opened the one dated September 26, 1942, and started to read again.

Camp Lee, VA
Sept 26, 1942

Dear Folks,
*   Well its Saturday nite and most of the fellows have gone to town but it is raining here so I'm being good and staying home. I wrote one letter and will have time for one more. It rained here all afternoon so it is nice and cool here now.*
*   That cake was really good thanks a lot. You asked about that one letter well I never reread them so I suppose they are full of mistakes but then you just have to consider the source and let it go at that...*

Hailey had been listening to Simon read when the part about re-reading made her think about school. "Hummm," she thought to herself, "that's probably why Mrs. Lacey makes us re-read all our stuff; to check to see if we have made any mistakes.

Simon continued to read the letter.

*   Well 3 weeks in the camp are gone and it gets better all of the time. You get better acquainted all of the time and learn how to get around and do things. We were out on the rifle range this afternoon and got rained out so we will go back for about 2 hours in the morning.*
*   Well one more week and I move. I won't leave the camp but just go to another company while I go to school. But I will write you my address when it changes but I will get my mail if you send it here. Have you got the silo filled yet? The corn down here only grows about 3 feet tall. The main crop is peanuts. And they really have a lot of them. Lots of Negros around here too.*

Simon stopped reading and looked at his friends. "Melissa, add this to the list of questions, please."

Melissa looked blankly at Simon and asked, "Add what to the list?"

"That word, Negros," Simon answered. "I don't know what that word means. I haven't heard it before." Melissa watched and listened to her friends as they all agreed that they had never heard the word before.

"You are kidding right, guys?" Melissa joked. The group of friends stared at Melissa, all shaking their heads and saying, no. Hailey knew by the look on Melissa's face that she knew something the rest of them did not.

"Well, just finish the letter, Simon, and I'll explain after," Melissa said quietly.

There is one little fellow comes up here every nite to shine shoes and he is always getting dates with his older sisters for us but we never go. Wonder why. He says that he is going to go in the navy. He says he's no army man. His name is Alexander Brown.

The colored folks down here seem to have a lot of respect for a white too. In buses they have to sit in the rear at all times. And then in restrooms up town they all have their own and some will not allow them in stores even.

Well it is getting late and I will write more tomorrow and try to write some of the rest back home. Say about the pickup I'm afraid that you would miss it and that is a good motor but suit yourself about it. I'll write more later.

Maynard

The friends sat motionless for what seemed like an hour to Hailey. When she looked around at their faces, Hailey noticed that they all looked as confused as she felt, all but Melissa. Hailey stared at Melissa's face for a long time trying to figure out what it was she knew. Melissa had her chin resting in her hand with her eyes all squinted up and her mouth closed in a tight line. Simon made Hailey jump when he interrupted the silence by asking Melissa what they all wanted to know. "So what gives, Lissa? What do all of those words mean and how come those...what were they...colored people...couldn't go into stores and had to use special bathrooms. Were they like green or purple or what? I don't get it."

Hailey watched as Melissa sat back in her chair and take a deep breath. It was several seconds before Melissa answered Simon's question. When she did, it was almost as if she didn't believe that the rest of her friends really didn't know what the letter was saying or what the words meant. "Come on guys, you are kidding, right?

"No, really," Joel confirmed. "I for sure don't understand what's going on in the letter."

"Okay, well then...," Melissa paused for just a second looking around at the faces of her best friends. "So, I'm gonna explain the colored folk thing first. You guys know that I'm African American, right, and sometimes people call us black."

"Yaaaa," they all answered.

Melissa continued, "Well back in those days they called African Americans Negros or colored."

"So that is like me being Asian and Rita and Simon being Irish. It's kind of like where you came from, right?" Blake asked.

"Well, sort of." Melissa answered.

"But what about the bus and bathroom and store and stuff?" Simon pressed.

Melissa sat thinking again. Hailey watched as she began to squirm in her chair. "What's the matter, Lissa?" She asked.

"Well," Melissa hummed, "this part is harder to explain, but I'll try." Melissa scooted up closer to the table and grabbed the letter that was now lying on the table. She scanned the last part of the letter quickly and slowly started to speak. "So, back then, like when my Grandma Sophie was a little girl, people were afraid or scared of different things or being different. She's told me stories about who she calls *'her people'*. I guess those would be her ancestors who actually came from Africa. She said that people went to Africa and captured black people and brought them to America and sold them to other people so that they would work on their farms or...plantations, that's what she called them."

"NO WAY!" Robin hollered. "That's not right. That's way wrong! You can't buy and sell people."

Hailey knew the whole group was in total shock. She asked what she knew the rest were thinking. "How could that possibly be true? How could that even happen?"

"I'm telling you guys, it is true, my grandma wouldn't lie." Melissa insisted. "Besides, my mom has stories, too, about...what's the word...oh yeah, discrimination. That's what the letter means about the colored folk or Negros having to use different bathrooms and sitting in the back of the bus." Melissa stopped and thought for a minute. "Tell you what," she piped up, "how about I ask my Grandma Sophie to come to the next meeting of the SSCH?"

"That would be way cool," Shelly agreed. "But I think we need to add discrimination to the list and maybe ask Mrs. Lacey to make it a word of the day so we can look it up, discuss it, and figure out exactly what it means." Shelly put Maynard's letter safely in the binder where she was writing all of their questions. Then she turned to a clean page, pulled it out of the binder, and set it in front of Robin. "Here, we already decided you have the beast handwriting out of all of us. You should write the invitation to Melissa's grandma."

Hailey watched as Robin wiggled the paper until she seemed to be satisfied with its position. Then she watched as

Robin reached for her backpack that was sitting on the floor next to her chair and pull out a whole wad of colored pencils and pens held together with a rubber band. "So, which one should I use," Robin asked, holding them up so the whole group could see them.

Rita was the first to respond. "PINK! I love pink, and she probably should use a pen, not a pencil."

"Really, come on Rita," Simon scolded. "Pink. She should probably use blue or black for the same reason she should use a pen. This is going to be a .... like a formal invitation for an adult. This isn't some girlie birthday invitation or scrapbook swirly, flowery thing." Simon looked around the table at the faces of his friends. He held his hands out in front of him with his chin jutted out and his eyes opened really wide looking for support.

Hailey couldn't help herself. She started to giggle. "I think for once you got her, Simon." She turned to face Rita so she could explain why she had sided with Simon. "Rita, ..."

"I know, I know, he's right ...but I still like pink." She paused. "Maybe we can draw pink flowery, swirly decorations on it, or use a pink envelope," she finished with a smirk and her tongue sticking out at her brother.

"Yeah, maybe," Simon agreed, to make his sister happy.

The group scooted closer to Robin so they could all see what she was writing. They all had ideas on what should be said and how to say it. They all knew what they wanted it to say; the only problem was how to say it. It took a long time and a lot of pieces of paper, but finally Robin had an invitation that had all the information on it and that they all liked. The invitation read;

Dear Mrs. Sophie Parks,

Hello, we are the members of the club called Super Secret Catacomb Hunters. Our clubhouse is in Hailey Burke's basement. That is where we hold our meetings. We

have been hunting through boxes and trunks in her basement for a few weeks and have found all kinds of cool stuff.

A couple of meetings ago we found a box full of letters from Hailey's great-grandpa to his mother and father. Today we found a letter that talked about things most of us don't get. The letter says things like "colored folk have to sit in the back of the bus." Melissa said that you know about this kind of stuff.

59

We were wondering if you could explain it to us. We would like to invite you to our next club meeting so that maybe you can help us understand what the letter is talking about. Our next meeting is next Saturday at 1:00 o'clock, at Hailey's house. If you can come, you can tell Melissa and then she can tell the rest of us.

Sincerely,

Robin Silverman
From the Super Secret Catacomb Hunters

Robin handed the letter to Rita. She read it and then pushed the letter to Blake to read. He passed it to the next person, who passed it to the next. Once they had all read it, they decided, even Rita, that it didn't need any flowers. This letter was too important and serious. Hailey sent Blake upstairs to ask her mom for an envelope. It only took Blake a couple of minutes to come back with an envelope that was pale pink. He handed it to Rita. She waved the envelope in the air and smiled at Simon. Then she handed it to Robin.

"I don't believe she got her way," grumbled Simon. "She always gets her way."

"Sorry dude, that's what Mrs. Burke had," Blake apologized. Simon just shook his head while the rest of the group laughed.

Robin put the letter in the envelope, licked the sticky part to seal it, and then handed it to Melissa. Melissa put it in the front pocket of her back pack to carry home and give to her Grandma Sophie.

Hailey noticed that it was almost time for everyone's parents to start coming to pick them up. She thought that it might be a good idea to maybe find stuff on their own, so she suggested it to her friends before they had to leave. They all thought it was a good idea, too. Even though they were going to ask Mrs. Lacey if they could choose the word "discrimination" as the word of the day on Monday, they agreed that it would be good to be prepared, so they thought about giving themselves some kind of homework. Hailey was the first to suggest a few words that they could look up on their own; words that they had already talked about today, words they didn't understand, words like colored folk and Negros, and of course the word discrimination. That way, she told them, they could show Mrs. Lacey how serious they were and how much they had already done. Each child took a piece of paper from the binder and wrote the three words Hailey had mentioned. "Don't forget to write down what you find out and anything else you might want to know," Hailey added.

"Hailey!" her mom called from the top of the basement stairs. "It's time to adjourn the meeting, kiddo. I've got moms and dads up here waiting to take kids home."

Hailey and her friends snickered. "Okay, Mom, we were done anyway. We're on our way up," she continued as they all made sure everything was neatly put away and in order for the following Saturday's club *SSCH* meeting. She and Blake were the last ones to come up on the lift. "Blake, you should be in charge of making sure the boys don't forget to bring their club homework to school," Hailey stated. "And maybe Shelly could be in charge of reminding the girls."

"Sure," both Shelly and Blake answered. "We can do that."

"Okay, cool," Hailey yelled as the children began to leave with their parents. "See you guys at school on Monday, then."

Hailey spent the rest of the afternoon and evening doing her real homework for school. She wanted to make sure she had it all done before she started on her other homework so she didn't get in trouble. That way she would have all day Sunday to work on her SSCH homework. Before she went to bed that night, Hailey had asked and

61

gotten permission to use the computer for most of the next day. She told her mom and dad what she and her friends had talked about that day and explained that everyone was going to look up the definitions of some words they didn't know too well. Hailey couldn't wait until morning. She was way curious and excited about what she might find.

Bright and early Sunday morning Hailey was up before her parents. She had already been awake for a while before she got out of bed. She had wanted to sleep in because it was Sunday, but she wanted to get to work on her project also. Besides, her head was too full of questions and words, and ideas and stuff to sleep anymore.

Once Hailey was dressed she quietly made her way to the kitchen where she made herself a bowl of Cheerios and a glass of orange juice. She really wanted to take it all into her dad's office where the computer was so she could eat and work at the same time. Hailey thought better of that idea and ate at the kitchen table. She could see herself trying to balance a bowl full of cereal and milk and a glass of juice while she drove her wheelchair through the living room. Then she pictured the bowl of cereal laying upside down on the new carpet and her mom standing there either yelling or crying. She couldn't figure out which would be worse. Either way, she'd be in trouble and feel bad. "Better safe than sorry," she thought to herself.

Done with her breakfast and her dishes in the sink, Hailey was sitting in front of the computer trying to type in one of the words on her list. It was the biggest word on the list and she wasn't sure how to spell it. She sounded out the word...d i s k r i m e n a sh un, as she typed it into the search engine. When she clicked on enter the computer asked her if she really wanted the word "discrimination". Hailey laughed at herself. "Whoa, that was way off. Thank goodness for smart computers and things like spell check." When she found a website that looked like it was sort of like a dictionary, Hailey clicked on the link. When it opened, she read what it said.

Discrimination noun

1. an act or instance of <u>discriminating</u>.

2. treatment or consideration of, or making a distinction in favor of or against, a person or thing based on the group, class, or category to <u>which</u> that person or thing belongs rather than on individual merit: *racial and religious intolerance and discrimination.*

3. the power of making fine distinctions; <u>discriminating</u> judgment: *She chose the colors with great discrimination.*

4. *Archaic* . something that serves to differentiate.

What she found was more than she could understand. She found a definition for the word discrimination, but it was too complicated. "Holy Moly," Hailey said out loud as she grabbed the top of her head and flung herself against the back of her chair. "How the heck am I supposed to figure this out? Look at all these other words that I don't know what they mean. This is gonna take me all day." Then she looked up another site hoping it would explain better or at least be easier to understand. There she found something that she understood a little bit better.

Discrimination is the <u>prejudicial</u> treatment of an individual based on their membership - or perceived membership - in a certain group or category. It involves the actual behaviors towards groups such as excluding or restricting members of one group from opportunities that are available to another group. It involves excluding or restricting members of one group from opportunities that are available to other groups.

She actually understood the part about how people behave toward other people. She was always being excluded or not being allowed to do things other people got to do. Hailey kept reading and found out that there were all kinds of discrimination. There was racial, religious, nationality, age, and the one she knew about, disability. On her first day at her new school she remembered the things some of the children said about her, and even to her. She knew it was only because they didn't know anything about her or about people with disabilities...at least not at first. Some of her new classmates had prejudged her because she was in a wheelchair, and because of what they heard their parents say about people who were disabled. Hailey sat for a few minutes remembering her first day of school. "Man, I'm glad that day is over," she said quietly, shaking her head back and forth.

Hailey didn't think many people in Monticello understood as well as people in California that all people were different. She didn't know why, she just did. Maybe Melissa's Grandma Sophie or Mrs. Lacey could explain. Hailey jumped at the sound of her mother's voice. "Hey, how long have you been up and what are you working on?"

"You scared me, Mom," Hailey answered. "I've been up a couple of hours, I guess. Before you ask, I already ate breakfast, my homework is done, and you guys said I could use the computer today, remember?'

"Yes, I do," Joan laughed. "But not all day. Let's wrap it up in a couple more hours, okay? It's too nice of a day to spend it totally inside."

"Okay, sure, Mom, but this is really interesting stuff, this stuff about discrimination, prejudice, and Melissa's grandma is going to come talk to us all about segregation, or I hope she is. We invited her to come to a club meeting," Hailey informed her mother. Then she shared with her mom what she had learned so far and that all her friends were doing the same SSCH Club homework getting ready for tomorrow when they were going to ask Mrs. Lacey if they could pick the word of the day and discuss it. She told her mom that the word they wanted to talk about was discrimination, but she figured that all kinds of others words were probably going to come up too; words that she had seen that morning, some she knew and some she didn't, like prejudice, intolerance, excluded, and scapegoat and stereotype.

Joan stood next to Hailey almost speechless. "My goodness," she finally mumbled. "All these questions and words and work all because of what you kids found in the basement? It's almost better than school, I think."

"I don't think so, Mom. We have questions but no answers, not yet anyway," Hailey joked. "We need a teacher to explain."

When Hailey was done with her computer research she put all of her notes and papers in a folder that she had labeled 'BOX FULL OF LETTERS'. Then she put the folder on top of her school binder so she didn't forget to take it to school the next day. She could hardly wait. Monday was going to be a really fun day. She could just tell.

Hailey didn't even make it off of the school bus before the members of the SSCH Club were trying to talk to her. She and Blake had already shown each other what they had found out about the words they had looked up while they rode the bus to school. Lots of it was the same, but some was different. She hoped the rest of her friends had done the homework, too. She thought it was going to be kind of fun and exciting to share and compare what they each had found. When she and Blake were finally off of the bus, Melissa held up a light blue envelope and waved it back and forth in front of the whole group. "Check it out," she taunted, jumping up and down. "Guess who is coming to our meeting on Saturday?"

"No way," Joel and Simon both shouted.

"Way," Melissa shrieked. "She said she would LOVE to. She said she would be honored."

"Woo-Hoo" The rest of them sung.

"Our first guest speaker. Oh, do we need to dress up?" Rita questioned. "Cause if we do, I think we need to go shopping," she finished as she flipped her hair over her shoulder.

The boys stared at Rita. Simon said one word to his sister: "REALLY?"

Hailey looked around at her friends and, trying to keep the peace, said, "No, I don't think so," but couldn't help snickering "but we can definitely dress nice." Luckily, the bell for school rang and saved Hailey from having to keep Rita from beating up her brother...again.

Once they were inside the classroom, Hailey waved Shelly to the back of the room where her desk sat. She whispered to Shelly, "Hey, you are the bravest and best talker, how about you ask Mrs. Lacey if we could do the word of the day today. Ya know, just like we talked about."

"Okay, but what if she wants proof that we are really serious?" Shelly questioned.

"No problem," Joel insisted, walking up behind Shelly. "We just show her all of our research and stuff," he finished, holding a handful of papers. "I really got into it, I mean it's kind of like the first day of class when we first met Hailey and didn't know anything about her and thought she didn't belong in our class 'cause she was different. And then we learned that everyone is different and no one is better than anyone else. And remember how we didn't think Blake was different than the rest of us because we forgot he wears hearing aids on account of we just got used to him having them?"

Blake and the other children had also gathered around Hailey's desk to listen to the conversation. When Joel finally stopped talking, Blake and Hailey looked at each other and started to laugh. "Man," Blake gasped, "Does he ever forget anything or ever stop talking?"

Everyone laughed. Out of the corner of her eye, Hailey watched as Mrs. Lacey made her way back to the where the group was standing. Hailey elbowed Shelly to get her attention by whispering, "Show time."

Hailey heard Shelly clear her throat and then smile up at Mrs. Lacey. She could also see that Mrs. Lacey was a little apprehensive. "So, what's going on back here?" Mrs. Lacey cautiously asked.

"Well, we were wondering if we could pick the word of the day because when we were at Hailey's house we found some things, some letters, that have words in them that we didn't understand and so we all decided," Shelly pointed around at each child in the group before she continued, "to do what do you call it, oh yeah, research, so we could figure out what they meant." Without taking a breath Shelly continued. "So can we?"

Mrs. Lacey stood silently only raising one eyebrow at Shelly. "Can we?" She repeated.

All of the children stared blankly at Mrs. Lacey. Robin, who was standing on the other side of Shelly, tapped her on the shoulder and mouthed the words *'may we'*. "Oh yeah, I mean may we pick the word?" Shelly corrected.

"I suppose so," Mrs. Lacey agreed. You seem to have come prepared. I'm impressed, but what brought all of this on? Wait…" Mrs. Lacey interrupted holding her hand up in front of her before her students could take charge. "Let's all take our seats and do this the right way; quietly, orderly, and organized."

The children made their way to their assigned desks. Once they were done with their first thing in the morning routine; flag salute, attendance, turning in homework, all that kind of stuff, Mrs. Lacey settled down in her chair with her hands folded on top of her desk. "So," she began, "who's going to explain to me the sudden interest in choosing the word of the day?"

Hailey and her friends sat looking at each other for a moment. No one was answering, so she decided to jump in and get the ball rolling. But before she could say anything, Simon blurted out, "Remember a couple of weeks ago when we had the word ancestor as the word of the day? Well, hummmm…well, after that we all went to Hailey's house and kind of went exploring in her basement where there's all kinds of cool old stuff like clothes, and toys and dishes," Simon paused, " oh yeah, and pictures and papers. Then we talked to Hailey's dad and he said that it all belonged to relatives, relatives that lived a long time ago and that those people were Hailey's ancestors. All the stuff belonged to Hailey's mom's family." Hailey listened as Simon finally stopped and took a deep breath.

Blake continued the story. "So, we were looking through everything, all the boxes and trunks, and found a shoebox of old letters that we started reading. They were like from 1942…"

Hailey sat back in her chair and was happy to let her classmates and fellow club members explain. She could see that Mrs. Lacey was really interested, too, especially when Blake got to the part about the letters. She saw Mrs. Lacey sit up taller in her chair and almost interrupt Blake but then change her mind. When Blake was done, Mrs. Lacey was quiet for what seemed like a very long time.

"My goodness, this is all very interesting. I'd love to see what you found," Mrs. Lacey finally said. "Hailey, you don't suppose your parents would let you bring them into school, do you?" She added looking in Hailey's direction.

Hailey startled at the mention of her name. "Ah, no but …"

Melissa threw her hand up in the air and excitedly started talking before she was called on. "No, but my Grandma Sophie is gonna come to our club meeting on Saturday and explain some things to us that were in one of the letters. Mrs. Lacey could come to the meeting, couldn't she, Hailey?"

"Sure, why not," she answered, shrugging her shoulders but thinking to herself that it might be kinda weird having her teacher come to her house, especially to a SSCH

Club meeting. "I can ask my mom." Then Hailey took the opportunity to finish what Simon had started. "That's why we wanted to know if we could pick the word for today and maybe for more than today, on account of we have a binder with words that we don't or didn't know what they mean. We all tried to look them up in the dictionary and on the computer and wherever else we could think of, but we need to know for sure if we got them right." Hailey stopped and bit her lip waiting for her teacher to answer. What she saw instead was a grownup who was way too excited about being invited to a kids club meeting. When Mrs. Lacey did answer, it was with a whole bunch of questions.

"Hailey, can you give me your phone number so I can call your parents and make sure it is alright for me to come over to your house on Saturday? What time is your meeting? Can I bring something; snacks or drinks? I guess we should get started on your words then, don't you? What are your words? What exactly is your grandma going to talk about Melissa? I can hardly wait; do you realize that those letters are almost one hundred years old?" Mrs. Lacey finished off her rant with a squeal and a clap of her hands.

"No, like seventy years old," Robin corrected seriously, which caused the whole class to erupt into laughter. "Well, it's true," she defended, holding her hands up beside her face palms up, her chin jutted out, and her eyes opened wide, "we already did the math, remember?"

Hailey knew Robin was right, but she still felt a little bad for her because when she was being serious people sometimes laughed at her. Robin was the kind of person that wanted everything perfect. Well, not always, but usually. That was why they had all wanted Robin to write the invitation to Grandma Sophie. They wanted it perfect. Robin was one of the quietest people Hailey had ever known, and it was good in some ways because you didn't have to worry about Robin being all hyper like her friend Joel. Mrs. Lacey interrupted Hailey's thoughts by asking the class who was going to go up to the whiteboard and write the words they wanted to discuss. Without missing a beat the whole class shouted out one name, Robin!

Robin proudly walked up to the board with papers from her classmates and their club binder and made a list of the words they wanted to study. It was a long list beginning with the word discrimination followed by the words prejudice, intolerance, Negro, colored folk, and scapegoat and stereotype.

"Wow," was all Hailey heard Mrs. Lacey say when Robin closed the binder and returned to her seat.

The whole class waited while Mrs. Lacey stood and looked at the words on the board. "I don't know what is in those letters you guys found, but I am definitely coming to your meeting," Mrs. Lacey joked. "Let's get started on word number one," she prompted. "Discrimination, what have you got?"

Since that was Hailey's word to look up, she raised her hand to speak. "So, this is what I found out about this word. It means like putting people down, or thinking someone is better than another person, or not letting them do things that other people get to do, like for example," Hailey stopped and thought for a second and then looked around the room. "Like when I first started going to school here and someone, I don't remember who, but someone said that I didn't belong here. They said that they didn't have kids like me at this school, people in wheelchairs. That person was discriminating against people in wheelchairs." Hailey looked around the room again and noticed that her friends' faces were all turning a funny color of red. When she realized that she had embarrassed them, she hurried to make them feel better. "Not to worry guys, I get that all the time. I was just using that as an example. And besides, when we got to know each other, it's like I don't even have a wheelchair anymore, most of the time anyway." Hailey could tell that she had helped her friends feel better. She sort of knew they had all sort of wanted to forget the first day of school. Then she thought of another example that might make them forget. "And remember girls, when we were first going to hang out and we didn't want to invite the boys because...well, because they are boys." Hailey snickered, "well, we were discriminating against them."

"Hey," the boys sung out. "What do you mean," Joel mumbled "that's not fair to cut us out of the action because we aren't girls."

"And that," Mrs. Lacey spoke up quickly to defuse any arguments, "is the perfect definition of discrimination."

During 'word of the day' time that week one of the words from the binder was written on the board by a different student each day. The class studied and discussed each one in detail just as Hailey had done on Monday with her word. Hailey thought it was really cool and was really proud that they had come up with the idea and that their teacher thought it was a good enough idea to use.

By Wednesday afternoon Hailey knew that Mrs. Lacey had called and talked to her mom about coming over on Saturday. Hailey even knew that Mrs. Lacey had asked if other teachers and parents could come over to listen to Grandma Sophie. After school Hailey's mom had shared the news with her. At first she was freaked. "EXCUSE ME," Hailey shouted after her mom explained that Mrs. Lacey had called and thought it would be a great learning experience for everyone, not just Hailey's friends. "That is just weird, Mom. Teachers aren't supposed to come to people's houses."

"Wait just a minute young lady," Joan scolded her daughter. "What was one of those words you talked about in class? And why can't your teacher come to your house to participate in certain activities."

Hailey sat stunned. "OMG...I can't believe I just did that. All of us, you know all of us in class and especially the SSCH Club, promised we were never gonna do that again, ever." She paused for several seconds and then added, "It is gonna be cool to have Grandma Sophie come talk to us, and I guess it would be kind of mean and rude not to ask Mrs. Lacey to come, especially since she knows about it and has been super interested in all of our words." Hailey slumped back in her chair, ashamed of what she had just said. Suddenly, she popped back up tall, holding onto the arms of her chair with her eyes big as saucers. "Hey, how did you know about the 'word of the day' anyway.?"

Joan laughed. "I have my ways."

By the time it was Saturday, Hailey and her family had decided that the basement might be too small for all the people who were going to show up for what her mom had called an activity. It seemed to her to be turning into an event or party. Since it was still kind of nice outside at this time of year, they had decided to set up a bunch of chairs out on their huge front lawn. Joan and Hailey had spent Friday evening making dozens of cookies; all different kinds. The rest of the club members were bringing stuff, too, like punch and cups, and napkins, and lots more stuff to eat. Blake and his family were the first to arrive. Since they lived just a few houses away from Hailey's, they had offered to come help set up. The Burke and the Nagareda families had become good friends even after Blake's mom had been afraid of Hailey, after she got used to Hailey and her wheelchair.

It wasn't too very long before other people starting arriving. Hailey's mom told everyone to help themselves to refreshments and to make themselves at home. Hailey and the SSCH Club members gathered together to go over their plan for what was going to happen while they waited for everyone to show up. They had decided that they were all going to stand up in front of everyone and explain how they found the letters, how they learned about some hard words, and how they wanted to learn more. Then Melissa would go get her grandma and bring her where they were while Hailey introduced her to the crowd of kids, parents and of course, the teachers.

Soon, Joan walked up to the circle of friends and ask, "What do you think guys? Looks like everybody is here. Do you think you should get this show on the road?"

"Probably," Simon agreed. "We don't want them to eat all the food and then leave. They gotta stay for the talk, 'cause it's gonna be really informative."

"What," the group said all at the same time.

"Informative? Where did you learn that word?" Rita questioned with her hand on her hip and one eye squinted closed.

"Ha ha," Simon chirped. "Mom said it when she found out we were doing this. Then she had to explain it to me so I would know. I know something you don't know, or at least I did, for a while," he sadly admitted.

The group headed to the spot in front of all of the folding chairs. When they had finished the speech they had been practicing, Melissa left the group and walked to where her Grandma Sophie was sitting in the front row. Grandma Sophie stood up and took Melissa's hand and walked with her until they returned to the center of the waiting children. Hailey rolled her wheelchair up to sit next to Melissa and her grandma. She cleared her throat and raised her right hand while she presented Grandma Sophie to the crowd. "This is Sophie Parks. She is Melissa's grandma, Grandma Sophie, and she is going to explain to us some of the stuff in the letters we just told you about. Some of the stuff we didn't get, things we couldn't figure out. And I guess all you guys didn't understand some of it either 'cause you're here to listen to Grandma Sophie, too. It must be pretty interesting stuff because Mrs. Lacey, our teacher, is here with some of the other teachers from school," she finished with a shrug of her shoulders. "So, we're all going to sit down now," pointing to herself and the club members, "so Grandma Sophie can start telling her story, or teach her lesson, or whatever."

Grandma Sophie chuckled as the group found seats. "Thank you for asking me to come talk to you all today. I am very proud to have been invited. I didn't know it was going to be such a big gatherin'. I'm a little flustered to have to speak to so many people at one time, but if you are willin' to listen, I'm willin' to tell some stories." Sophie settled down into the big chair the children had decorated for her and began. Well, this sure is a mighty fine lookin' chair." She said rubbing her hands back and forth on the big overstuffed cushions. "I don't think I've ever seen one so nice."

Hailey looked at Melissa, and they both smiled. She heard the audience giggle and saw everyone kind of relax after Grandma Sophie said what she did. Hailey thought that was pretty smart of Grandma Sophie; to say something funny first before she started getting serious. It seemed to her that it made everyone happy and ready to listen. Even Joel was sitting still on the ground in front of the first row of chairs with his elbows resting on his crossed knees and his chin resting in his hands. "Like always," Hailey thought to herself. "He's not going to miss a thing."

"Well," Grandma Sophie began again. "I suppose ya'll are here for the same reason. To hear me tell a little story. A story 'bout when I was just a youngun'." She paused. "I have a question for you first. Who here can tell me the name of the President of the United States?"

Hailey and all of her friends yelled out the answer. They knew who the President was and that he was kind of important because he was the first black person to ever be President.

"Alright then, I think I'm sittin' amongst some right smart folks," Grandma Sophie joyfully stated. "Kind of keep that in the back of your minds, on the back burner so to speak, while I share some things and answer some questions these children asked me in a right fine letter invite." Grandma Sophie cleared her throat and leaned back in the soft chair. "So, first off, let me tell ya'll that I was born in the year nineteen hundred and forty-nine in Biloxi Mississippi, not too far off from that Kessler Air Force Base. But that's a whole 'nother story," she chuckled to herself shaking her head. "Back in that time we was called somethin' different than we're called today. Today I'm known as a Black person or even an African American. Back then I was colored folk or Negro. These kids here asked me what those words meant so I'm here to tell 'em. They also wanted to know what segregation was about. I'm here to tell 'em that, too. So let's get started.

"Back way before I was born, before my mama's mama was born, more'n almost four hundred years ago, some of my ancestors were brought to America from Africa by people who were called slave traders. So ya'll know, traders were people who sailed on ships and bought and sold all kinds of things like sugar, salt, things to sew with, you name it, they brought it to America from wherever it was made. But I have to tell ya'll, too, slavery was goin' on long before the first slave traders brought slaves to America. Ya see, my first ancestors in America were slaves.

"Africa was like any other place. There were many different towns, or groups, or tribes, whatever you choose to call them, and they had slaves. Most people believe that slaves were stolen or caught by the slave traders. But in the beginnin', this just wasn't true. Most slaves, in the beginnin', were bought by white people from other African people. Most often, the winnin' or strongest tribes sold into slavery the people belongin' to the tribes that they captured during wars. It wasn't until some time later that the traders, the slave traders, took to goin' to Africa to buy or kidnap' African people themselves, and stole them away from their families and homes, and brought them to America to sell them to other people, mostly white people I'd say."

"Whoa, wait just one second," Joel stammered jumping to his feet and running toward Grandma Sophie. "You can't buy and sell people. They aren't houses, or dogs or ...or ..."

"Or property," Grandma Sophie supplied.

"Yeah! Like property. People aren't property," Joel insisted, throwing his arms in the air and looking around at all the faces of all the people sitting in the yard listening to Grandma Sophie.

Joel's parents jumped to their feet looking a little embarrassed. They both ran to Joel and tried to console him and apologize to Sophie. Hailey wasn't sure why they looked embarrassed. She figured they should be used to him doing that kind of thing. It was just the way he was, just the way it was. Then she heard Grandma Sophie say the words she had just thought in her own head.

"You are right, Joel. In the world you know, in the year two thousand and twelve, people are not property. Nor can you buy or sell them. But back then, before any of us were even born, that was just the way it was."

Joel stood perfectly still. It was several seconds before he even moved. When he did move it was to scratch the top of his head. Hailey knew he did that if he didn't understand or if he did understand and wanted to know more about something. "So, what happened to the people who the slave traders sold to other people?" Joel asked.

Bluntly, Grandma Sophie answered Joel's question. "They became property." After a long minute Sophie continued. "They became slaves to big plantation owners."

After another shorter pause she continued. "The slave traders didn't just steal people from their families and homes; they helped the plantation owners steal their history, their identity. You might ask how that could happen. Well, since the people from Africa were the property of plantation owners, they could pretty much do what they wanted with them. They took everything the African people knew; their names, their traditions, their language, and their freedom. Lands sakes, these people from Africa didn't even know where they were much less what was happenin' to them. And I can bet ya'll know that when you get scared of something you tend to get skittish and quiet. The plantation owners took advantage of that very thing and did what you call *dehumanize* them. That sort of means makin' someone feel like less than a person, real unimportant." Sophie tried to explain. "They all but destroyed their value as people and turned them into something no better than a shovel. Why back then, in the beginnin', Negro slaves were forbidden to even learn to read or write."

Hailey was awakened from her state of concentration when she heard a gasp from behind her. When she turned around to look, she saw the strangest look on all of the adults' faces. When she turned to look back up at Grandma Sophie, she noticed the super serious expression on her face.

"I'm tellin' it as I know it," she defended. "Ya'll know that names are an important thing, whether they be positive or negative." Sophie stopped and reached over to pick up the glass of punch that someone had brought for her. She took a long drink, set the glass down, and took a deep breath. "I was sure gettin' dry," she joked. "So, names," she started again, "I'm thinkin' that the plantation owners didn't want the slaves rememberin' their history, where they came from on account of some of them slaves were royalty in their countries. They didn't want the slaves getting what they called "uppity" and out of control. I'm thinkin' that's why they came up with the name 'Negro' for the slaves."

Sophie stopped again and smiled looking up to the sky. Everyone else looked up, too, even Hailey. She didn't know why but she did it anyway. She looked back at Grandma Sophie. Hailey decided this was probably how Grandma Sophie pondered. Her dad said people pondered in different ways.

"So, we were talking about names and words." Hailey heard Grandma Sophie finally say. "I don't really know where the words Negro and colored came from. I've heard stories over the years, but I don't know if any of 'em are true. Maybe you children can do some research and find out for sure. Maybe your teacher can help you out with that. Anyway, I've been told that the word Negro is a Spanish word for black. I'm thinkin' some of the slave traders spoke that language. Spanish came from another older language called Latin. I don't know nothin' about Latin," Sophie declared throwing her hands up in the air, making everyone laugh," but I was told that in the old Latin language there was a word 'necro' that means dead." I also heard tell the first slaves came from a place near the River Negro somewheres in South America." Sophie stopped again and just looked at the people sitting in front of her. "Think for a minute what I was just tellin' ya'll and what you children wanted to know."

Out of the corner of her eye Hailey saw Robin very slowly raise her hand and wait for Grandma Sophie to call on her. "Yes, sugar, do you have a question?" Sophie asked.

"No," Robin answered quietly. "I have an answer." Everyone chuckled for just a second but Robin didn't stop. "You asked us to think about what we asked and what you just told us. I think the name the plantation people gave the African people was because they didn't want them to remember their past. They wanted it to not be there, like dead. And since their skin is darker, I don't think it's really black though, the Spanish word kind of fits, too."

"That was my guess," Sophie agreed. "And I'm not sure either why black folks started bein' called colored folks. My take on the whole situation is this," Sophie said scooting to the edge of the chair, leaning one elbow on her knee and shaking a finger at the whole group, "I think those white plantation owners figured they were a better kind of people than the slaves they owned. I think they thought we were lower than dirt. I think the plantation owners wanted to hold us down, keep us separate from themselves, and make us feel poorly about ourselves. And what better way to do that than call the black slaves 'colored' which was exactly the opposite of what they called themselves." Hailey jumped when Grandma Sophie suddenly snapped back up in her chair to continue. "I think it boils down to them tryin' to take our dignity away. And I can't think of a better way than to call us something as far away from white as they could think of."

81

Sophie ended her speech with a sharp nod of her head as she slid back in her chair.

Hailey realized that she had been sitting there for several seconds without breathing. When Grandma Sophie stopped talking she heard everyone around her take a giant gulp of air just like she had. Hailey suspected that they had all been listening so hard to Grandma Sophie that they had forgotten to breath, too, and then when she stopped talking, they all remembered again.

Hailey thought Grandma Sophie was a really good story teller. She was glad the Club had invited her to come. She was even glad Mrs. Lacey and all of the other teachers and parents had come, too. Hailey even thought that her Great-Grandpa Maynard would have learned something from hearing Grandma Sophie talk because she knew that everyone here was learning a lot. In the middle of her thought, Hailey heard Shelly and Rita mumbling behind her. It wasn't long before Rita stood up and asked Grandma Sophie a question. "Me and Shelly were just talking and we remembered that we learned in science, or someplace, that black was when all of the colors were not there and white is where all of the colors are there."

Shelly pulled on Rita's hand. When Rita bent down, Shelly whispered in her ear. Yeah, black reflects color and white absorbs colors." After a pause she added, "All colors. We think they had the whole thing wrong."

Hailey looked from the girls to Grandma Sophie and watched a big smile creep across her face. "I agree. I think they had it wrong, as well," she answered with a nod.

"Grandma," Melissa asked. "Can you tell us about the last word on our list?"

Which one is that, sugar?" Sophie answered.

"Look here in the binder Grandma," Melissa said, running up to her grandmother with it opened up in her hands. "This one..."

"Segregation," Sophie said out loud. "Thanks honey, we'll get to that right now."

Melissa hurried back to her seat so her grandmother could begin.

"Segregation," Sophie repeated. "Well, we kinda been talkin' about that already. It has to do with keeping people apart. Sometimes when you think you are better than someone else, you don't want them around. Sometimes you're just afraid of other people because they are different than you. Remember those slaves? Well, after a while, they did start to learn to read and write. After a while, they got to feelin' more comfortable about living in America. After a while, they wanted to be part of the new world they had come to." Sophie paused and Hailey watched her think. Then Sophie started again. "In the beginning there were laws about havin' slaves. People could own them, like we said before, like property. But after something called the Civil War that changed. There weren't supposed to be any more slaves, that was the new law. That law was called The Emancipation Proclamation."

Isn't that a good thing?" Blake asked.

Sophie laughed. "You'd think so, but white folk back then, mostly people from the South, didn't think so. The were still thinkin' they were better than black folk, and maybe they were a little mad because they got their property taken away. They were thinkin' that things should stay the same, and so, new laws were passed, laws like somethin' called The Jim Crowe Law." Sophie held up her hand to let everyone know that she was going to stop. Hailey could tell that she wasn't done though. She was just reaching behind her to get something. It was a book. When Grandma Sophie turned around, she opened the book to where she had marked it.

"I'm goin' to read this to ya'll because it explains it pretty well.

<u>Jim Crow laws</u> *were state and local laws in the* <u>United States</u>.

They were laws between 1876 and 1965. They required <u>segregation</u> in all public facilities, with a supposedly "<u>separate but equal</u>" status for black Americans. In reality, this separation led to treatment, financial support and accommodations that were usually inferior to those provided for <u>white Americans</u>.

"Now," Sophie said looking up. "Before you ask, I'm goin' to read something else because ya'll are going to ask what separate but equal means. So here goes."

<u>Separate but equal</u> *was a legal doctrine in <u>United States constitutional law</u> that allowed and justified services, facilities and public accommodations to be separated by race, on the condition that the quality of each group's public facilities was to remain equal.*

Joel raised his hand and waved it in the air. "None of that makes any sense. How come they made laws like that? What's the problem with people being different? What's the problem with people being different and eating at the same restaurant or, or, or" he stumbled. "Or using the same drinking fountain or bathroom. Everyone knows there's no such thing as cooties." Joel turned to stare at the girls sitting together. "Or like not getting invited to hang out because you aren't a girl."

"Sorry." The girls all said.

"I have to agree with you young man," Sophie replied. "And so does something called the Civil Rights Movement."

The what?" Joel asked.

"That's gettin' a little over my head and yours, sonny. All you really need to know is that people seemed to have seen the error of their ways and changed their minds, attitudes and laws about such things."

Hailey raised her hand to ask a question and when Grandma Sophie nodded her head, Hailey began. "So that's why we can all go to the same school and ride on the same bus like me and Blake, and eat in the same McDonald's, and all that kind of stuff? Because people started to think more like Joel?"

Grandma Sophie smiled, "Yep, and when people stop looking at what color skin is..."

"Or if your in a wheelchair or not," Hailey interrupted.

"Or if your in a wheelchair or not," Sophie added, "you can see what else a person's got. What they have on the inside." Sophie took a deep breath and Hailey noticed she was looking past everyone sitting in front of her. "America has come a long way," Grandma Sophie almost whispered. "I mean gosh-a mighty, from slave to President."

The whole group stood and clapped for a really long time. Grandma Sophie bowed slightly and said thank you for letting her come and talk.

When the clapping stopped, Hailey turned to her father and goaded. "See Dad, I told you. People can totally fight and change the establishment. Grandma Sophie just told us so."

Hailey's Family Tree

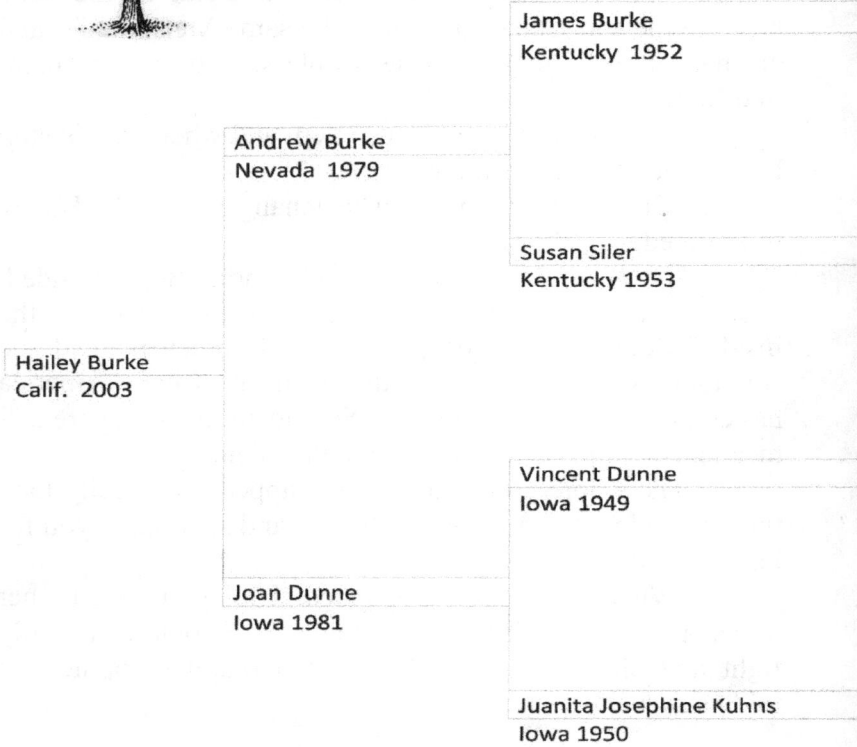

James Burke
Kentucky 1952

Andrew Burke
Nevada 1979

Susan Siler
Kentucky 1953

Hailey Burke
Calif. 2003

Vincent Dunne
Iowa 1949

Joan Dunne
Iowa 1981

Juanita Josephine Kuhns
Iowa 1950

	Michael Burke
Morgan Burke	NC 1897 Kentucky 1975
Kentucky 1930	Bridget Fry
	Virginia 1899 Tenn. 1971
	Benjamin Huddleston
Lucinda Huddleston	Virginia 1899 Tenn. 1981
Tenn. 1932	Sarah Elizebth Reynolds
	Tenn. 1910 1984
	Hiram Siler
John Siler	Tenn. 1965 Ky. 1954
Kentucky 1899-1997	Hannah Fry
	NC 1867 Ky. 1953
	John Owens
Flora Owens	Kentucky 1880-1978
Kentucky 1900-1997	Susan Tye
	Tenn. 1881 Ky. 1983
	Frederick Dunne
Michael Dunne	Ireland 1897 Iowa 1978
Iowa 1914-2000	Lillian Wilkins
	Iowa 1911-1982
	Thomas MaGill
Ann MaGill	NY 1899 Iowa 1976
NY 1903 Iowa 1981	Mary Mcguire
	Ireland 1909 Iowa 1973
	Harry Kuhns
Maynard Kuhns	Germany 1915 Iowa 1970
Iowa 1919-1952	Johanna Harms
	Germany 1897 Iowa 1966
	George Mennis
Helen Mennis	Iowa 1892-1968
Iowa 1921	Geraldine Hennessey
	PA 1890 Iowa 1977

**Hiram Siler birthdate should be 1865 – sometimes descendents make error when copying information.

87

Jennifer Kuhns

Hailey's Scrapbook

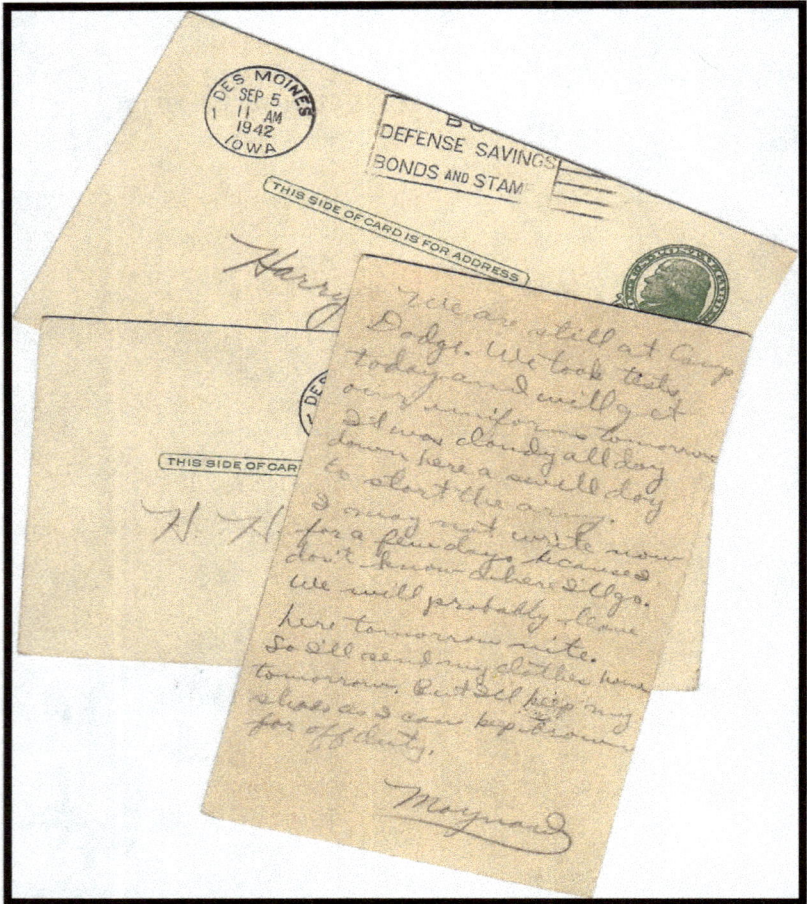

Vincent Dunne, Juanita Josephine Kuhns
with Joan Dunne Burke (as a baby)

Maynard Kuhns and Helen Mennis married
November 14, 1944

Geraldine Hennessey

George Mennis

Harry Kuhns and Johanna Harms Kuhns
50th Wedding Anniversary

The <u>REAL</u> Maynard Kuhns

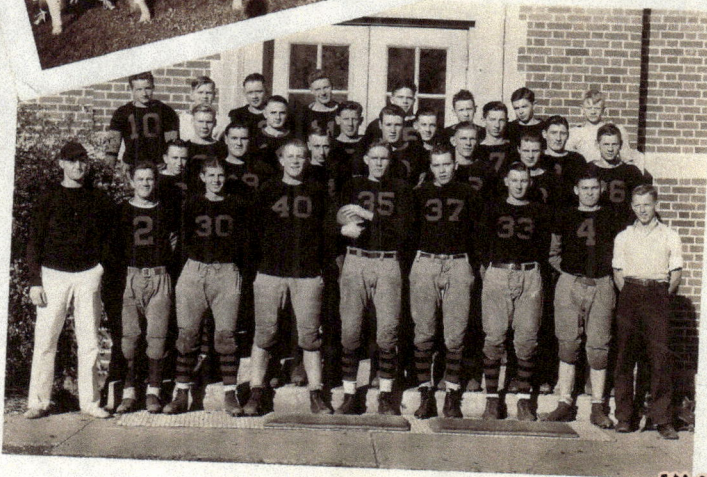

Maynard and Helen

Jennifer Kuhns

Maynard on the farm

ALSO BY JENNIFER KUHNS

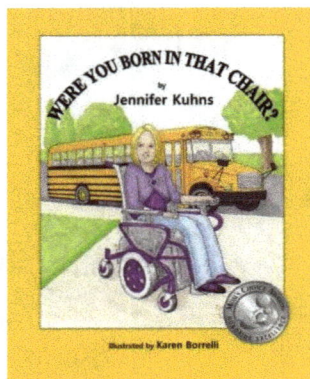

Shalako Press

http://www.shalakopress.com

www.ingramcontent.com/pod-product-compliance
Lightning Source LLC
Chambersburg PA
CBHW072151020426
42334CB00018B/1957